I0567946

The Good Word:
A Decade of
Jewish Thought and Chutzpah

David Bornstein

Copyright © 2013 David Bornstein

All rights reserved.

No Bards Invited Publishing
ISBN-13: 978-0615866383
ISBN-10: 0615866387

Dedication

This book is dedicated to my wife Patricia, who has always been
my life's most insightful editor and consultant, to my children
Ethan, Jerica, and Gabriel, who continue to be my best teachers,
and to my brother Ray who passed away in 2006, who encouraged,
challenged, laughed, and screamed at my words,
but in the end was always by my side.

TABLE OF CONTENTS

Acknowledgments

Cover art by Liana Finck

All photography by David Bornstein

Thanks to the editors at The Heritage Jewish News, who have
let me publish my heart and mind, and the community of
readers who have been supportive, critical and willing to voice
their opinions (almost) as readily as I.

Introduction

Like many things in life, my weekly column in the local Jewish newspaper began as an accident. More precisely, it began as a manipulation by my father, of which I was completely unaware.

My father was one of the grand old men of the Central Florida Jewish community. He helped create agencies and synagogues. He was viewed (and still is, many years after his death) as a pillar of Jewish ethics, a voice of reason, criticism, and wisdom. When he was offered a seat on the local Jewish Federation's Community Relations Committee late in his life, he saw it as more of a token gesture than a meaningful position, and he offered the spot to me, his disaffected, disconnected, avowed opponent of organized religion son. I took it on a lark, just to see what the Jewish world I'd left behind was made of.

That was in the late 1980s. Shortly thereafter, he passed away after a long battle with cancer, and I slowly, grudgingly, became more and more involved in our uniquely struggling, vibrant community, and began a search for who I was and what I believed that was based, not on esoteric philosophies or hallucinogenic experiences or fringe movements, but on a foundation of core Jewish teachings and values.

In 2000, after a decade of volunteer service, I became president of our local Jewish Federation, and in an attempt to communicate more widely and more positively with the greatest number of people possible, I wrote monthly columns for the local Jewish newspaper, the Heritage Jewish News. Many of these were simple reports on what was going on in and around Jewish Central Florida, but some of them were also explorations into the motivation for tikkun olam - for changing the world positively, for tzedakah - charitable giving, for volunteerism, for support of Israel, support of peace, and support, ultimately, for accepting and understanding who we are as Jews and human beings.

The reception was largely positive, and after my term ended the column continued, renamed The Good Word – Milah HaTovah. Given that the Heritage was willing to print virtually anything I submitted, I began casting a broader net, writing about everything from local agency issues to global politics, from personal, introspective pieces to questions about God and existence. I wrote articles on topics as general as holidays, peace and terrorism, economics, dogs, baseball, the follies of aging and the wisdom of youth, as long as somehow, somewhere, I could tie it back in to a Jewish context. I claimed no expertise, but I was willing to espouse my opinion on just about anything that came to mind.

In Hebrew, the number 18, or chai, is also the word for life, which is why 18 and its derivatives are considered lucky numbers. This collection of 72, or 4 lifetimes of brief essays, is all about seeing the Jewish world through the narrow lens of my eyes. But I hope it's also something a little more than that. I hope it's a snapshot of a time, a window open to a world of slightly offbeat possibilities, a permission slip to ask any question at any time.

The opinions expressed herein are those of the writer and not the Heritage Jewish News or any other individual, agency or organization. But if they evoke a response from you, whether it's a wince or a smile, then the journey has been worth the holes in my shoes. And that's The Good Word.

2002

Messages In The Western Wall

Who He Is

I am sitting near the front during Kol Nidre services, so close up that I'm aware of the Rabbi's gaze whenever he looks my way, aware of the whispers around me, aware of my children's fidgeting. My wife is sitting in the front row, waiting to be called on to do a responsive reading. She's been up there for nearly 45 minutes, and I'm alone with my 12-year old son on one side and my 9-year old daughter on the other. My daughter has her fingers wrapped in the strands of my talit. My son plays with a hairpin he pulled off a yarmulke. They're trying to be good, but I'm conscious of their every move. "Be still," I want to say. "Be quiet. Be invisible." I think about the times she messes with her brother's hair and teases him, and how stubborn she is and how sometimes it seems her favorite expression is "Nyeh." And I think about how he wakes up screaming that he can't go to school, and how quick he is to yell in my face and tell me I'm wrong. And I think about how often I want to strangle them both (metaphorically, of course). And then my daughter rests her head on my shoulder, and my son turns and kisses me, and all my thoughts evaporate as I remember I'm sitting in shul on the High Holy Days, and a strange peace settles over me and I'm left wondering why I was so uptight, and what my role is with them as a father and a Jew. This is what came to mind.

A father is always there. After work and on the weekend. Through the mumps, measles, and mono. A father lets his children know he is there for them forever and always.

A father knows that he is human. He makes mistakes. He loses his temper. He flies into neurotic fits. He admits that he's blown it, to himself and his children. And it's ok. He's not God. He's a man. He learns humility, and he passes it on.

A father sets the moral tone. Honesty, integrity, the 10 Commandments. He establishes standards of right and wrong in his household, and first and foremost, he lives by them so he can teach by example.

A father teaches forgiveness and consequences. He does two things at once: lets them know that there are consequences for their actions, and that as they accept those consequences they are forgiven completely. We continue our Jewish heritage as judges and teachers. They learn responsibility.

A Jewish father raises Jewish children. Lighting candles on Shabbat. A Jewish education, whether it's at a Hebew Day School, a Sunday school, Hebrew school, or at home. Celebrating our holidays. He cannot call himself a Jewish father unless he actively (key word) raises his children as Jews, reinforcing who they are in a non-Jewish world.

A Jewish father aspires to be more. My father always talked about how he wanted to be a general in the Israeli army. When he wasn't it didn't matter. He had dreams and aspirations. Our commitment to dream - of a homeland after World War II, of acceptance by the world, achievement in science and art and music, brings us closer to the perfection of God and makes us good role models and Jewish dads.

A Jewish father is accepting and hopeful. That his children will marry Jews. That if they don't their spouses will convert. That if they don't convert their children will. That if none of this occurs their grandchildren will still know their Jewish roots. That finally, if all else fails, they can look back and say they tried, and that their children grew up to be good human beings.

A Jewish father questions everything. Was I patient enough? Kind enough? Generous enough? Did I show how much I love them? Should I have been stricter? More lenient?

Set boundaries? Been more flexible? Do they know their history? Their backgrounds? Did I help them get secure in their Jewishness? If through questioning himself he changes and improves, it was all worth it.

A Jewish father is a Jew. To be a role model in his home he must first accept who he is. He doesn't shy away from proclaiming to the world, "I am a Jew," instilling Jewish pride as he does so. He may be religious or a purely cultural Jew. He may keep kosher or eat bacon for breakfast. He may put on tefillin or think davening is how you find water underground. But he understands, in his core, that he is a Jew, and his children know this and see and hear and touch and feel it someway every day. And when he does understand, with his children beside him, whispering, fidgeting, loving, it's then the kisses on Kol Nidre have a deeper meaning, and each New Year brings light and hope.

Tough Talk On The Middle East

Some of my most difficult conversations about Israel occur with my brother Ray. Ray feels that he was misled by our parents, privy to only one side of the Arab-Israeli conflict growing up. "I believe the main thing driving the Mideast conflict is attitude. Attitude on both sides, Arab and Jew. What I perceive to be skewed attitudes. So whenever I run into it, I react and work against it," he wrote me in a recent e-mail. He goes further: "I totally support the existence of the state of Israel, and I totally support its right to exist peacefully, without terrorist threat. At the same time, I totally support the desires of the Palestinian people for a nation of their own. I see their anger, their frustration, and while I do not condone or support their hatred and their terrorist groups, I do feel compassion for their suffering."

When Israel recently bombed an apartment building to kill a terrorist leader, also killing many innocent children in the process, Ray used this as proof that Israel doesn't just demolish empty buildings, but sometimes acts as viciously as the homicide bombers. He believes the "moral superiority" of Israel, the targeting of buildings vs. the targeting of civilians vanished in this act. And he feels that Israel's intimidation of the Palestinians, the squalor and economic oppression in which they live, is in itself an act of violence against humanity. He is so frustrated by the situation that his solutions include leveling Jerusalem if it remains a contentious issue, paying reparations to Palestinians who have lost their homes, and abandoning all settlements.

Alan Ginsburg, one of the philanthropic leaders of our community, recently invited me and my wife Pat to attend a dinner of local Jewish and Palestinian leaders. The short term goal: to talk, to build bridges by putting a face on the other side, and to potentially, over time, create relationships and friendships that could moderate the differences and allow real communication and understanding to take place. The long term goals: to start a Seeds of Peace chapter locally, to think of solutions for the problems in the Middle East, to start affecting change by taking a proactive stance at home. The evening was not designed to be political or confrontational. Unfortunately, as one might expect, politics intervened.

I sat at a table with an elder statesman of the Arab community, who has lived in the United States for many years, a bright, retired engineer who was obviously positional in his defense of the Palestinian people. While he talked about the violence halting on both sides, was vehemently opposed to the homicide bombers, and readily admitted that Arafat and Sharon both have to go, he kept sliding in messages about how understandable it is for Palestinians to revolt when they are hungry, malnourished, under curfew and generally oppressed. I listened quietly, choosing not to begin a dialogue with confrontation.

I've come away from these discussions with my brother Ray and my new contacts in the Arab community with new thoughts. First, it's vital that open debate take place, for creative solutions, perhaps, ultimately, for empathy by both sides. Second, it's equally vital that the Jewish community participate in public forums, regardless of how we feel about Israel. The Arab community outnumbered the Jewish community 2:1 at the dinner, and many of the Jews there were what I'd call eagerly conciliatory. Our Jewish backbone was represented minimally, and that embarrassed me. The same has been said of Seeds of Peace, that its membership has become largely Palestinian and is in danger of turning into a mouthpiece for Palestinian views. If that's the case, shame on us for allowing it. Jewish voices must be heard, and our presence felt.

And most difficultly, I believe we must be honest with ourselves. If we are to truly take the high moral ground we must be able to admit that the issues of the Middle East are grey, not black and white. Israel has made mistakes, and we can admit when Israel is wrong. A Palestinian state, is, I feel, an inevitability. The bombing of an apartment building was an error in judgment, a colossal, morally questionable error in judgment. Taking innocent lives, whether by accident or as casualties of war, is unconscionable. And yes, I believe the Palestinian support of homicide bombers is also unconscionable. But for real change to take place, we must rid ourselves of myth and misinformation, look deeply in the mirror of our souls, see our strengths and feel shame at our communal errors, and for the sake of humanity, make peace.

David Bornstein

A Plan For The Middle East

The following opinions may be controversial and stir emotions. You won't like everything I'm about to write. You'll probably agree with some points and disagree with others. Many of these ideas have been gleaned from correspondence and communication with others, so this is a shorthand synthesis, but like Moses striking the rock, you never know what may come out of it. That being said, I have a plan for change, not peace, in the Middle East.

First, and most central of all, nothing can occur until Palestinians and Arab nations all acknowledge Israel's right to exist forever. That's the only possible first step. After listening to Daniel Pipes, historian, political commentator, president of the Middle East Forum, and publisher of its Middle East Quarterly journal, I have come to the firm belief that the Palestinians really don't want Gaza and the West Bank. They want Gaza, the West Bank, and Israel, and they're currently convinced, in a war of attrition, that they can achieve this goal. Barak offered them a homeland, and they didn't just turn it down. They ignored the offer entirely. Snuff out any hope of the dissolution of the Jewish State. Israel exists. Period.

Second, Jerusalem is the capital of Israel, not Palestine. There is no good reason for Palestinians to claim Jerusalem as theirs. When Jerusalem was part Jordanian, Jewish holy sites were closed, desecrated, fouled. As an Israeli city, Jerusalem has been open to the world, excavated and invigorated, imbued with its true holy spirit. Jerusalem has modest importance to Muslims, but this isn't reason enough to make it the new Palestinian capital. The best I can see, Palestinians are using this as a thorn to irritate and antagonize, and nothing else. Let them choose from Jericho, Bethlehem, Hebron, wherever, but leave Jerusalem alone. It belongs to Israel.

Third, Israel ought to call a one-year hiatus on all forms of contact with Palestinians. This includes retaliation, further growth of the settlements, military incursions, all negotiations and discussions, and economic stimulation. It isn't going to be easy. First the borders would have to be tightly secured. The only Palestinians allowed in Israel would have to have work visas checked daily. There would be no back and forth travel otherwise. If Palestinians crossed the border they would be arrested or shot. The same would hold for Israelis. No protection if they cross the line. If terrorists snuck through Israel would kill them but not otherwise retaliate. On day one of the ceasefire a warning would be issued. Stop the violence and use the time for cooling off. If the one-year period is relatively quiet and items one and two have been agreed upon, negotiations for a Palestinian State would commence. If terrorist activity continued, on day 366 the Israeli Army would use all force necessary to obliterate all elements of Arab/Palestinian opposition and annex Gaza and the entire West Bank. Economic assistance could come from the rest of the world, and would be encouraged, not halted in any way. But the Palestinians must create a viable economy of their own. Hopefully they would thrive. If they remain in poverty due to their own poor leadership, but not due to Israeli curfews or destruction of property, tough. They have to figure out how to live on their own. It's not Israel's problem.

Fourth, there is no right of return, but reparations would be made in the form of the settlements. They would be turned over lock, stock, and barrel to the Palestinians. Which leads to #5, all settlements must go. The Palestinians need homes, and cannot govern a swiss cheese nation. Give them the settlements as final and complete payment for destroyed homes, and pull back.

And finally, create secure borders. Israel must be able to defend itself. Does that mean retaining the Golan? Does it mean a five or ten kilometer demilitarized zone? Does it mean annexing a certain amount of territory so the borders are more easily defended? I don't know, but I don't believe the pre-1967 borders work, and I don't think Israel needs more turf to feel secure.

I don't care who leads who, or whether or not the Palestinians have a democracy. I don't think those issues really matter. I think Israel needs security, and the Palestinians need to get real. Daniel Pipes said he didn't think anything would happen for another 20 or 30 years. I don't know anything other than that I pray for change. It's the only thing that makes sense in a senseless Middle East.

The True Meaning Of The Holidays

A Methodist child, a Lutheran child, and a Jewish child were discussing the holidays. The Methodist child said, "We go to church Christmas morning and then come home and open our presents. The Lutheran child said, "We go to church Christmas Eve and then open our presents first thing Christmas morning. The Jewish child said, "We celebrate differently We all go to my father's store, hold hands and sing Thank you Jesus for Christmas!"

When Pat and I first got married we rarely discussed religion or community. She grew up a humanist, without a connection to church or Christianity. I had lost my connection to Jewish Orlando, other than the occasional High Holiday obligation with my parents. We didn't know when we'd have kids, so how we raised our imaginary children didn't matter a whit.

During the winter when we visited Pat's family we celebrated Christmas with them. It was about as non-religious a holiday as there could be. No church. No Jesus. No crosses. Just a big turkey dinner and the traditional wake up early in the morning for presents orgy. It was fun.

One winter down here her family came to visit and we put up a Christmas tree. We wanted them to feel at home, and didn't want their holiday to seem cold and hollow. My father looked through a different lens. He saw his Jewish son compromising his integrity and beliefs to make his in-laws feel good. A man of principles, he refused to come in to the house. He had to make a statement, and did so with disdain. In the process, both Pat and I were hurt, no more so, in all likelihood, than he was when he found out we'd put up the ignoble tree in our living room. It took years to mend those fences, but they were mended, and years later, when we had children, we also had the important discussions about how to raise them (as Jews), and today we are a Jewish family, with no Christmas tree and multiple menorahs.

Now I am committed to my Jewishness and my Jewish community. I disapprove of the apologist, acculturating Jews who erect the unfortunate Chanukah bush for no good reason other than to make themselves feel as worthy as a Christian. What hogwash! What a waste.

Chanukah is a minor holiday, made huge by our materialism and our self-inflicted competition with Chrismas. But you know what? There's no good reason to compete. What's important to me, what I'm trying to convey to my children, is that the true meaning of the holidays isn't what we get. It's not even about what we give. It's how we look beyond ourselves and embrace others.

You see, I've always wondered why it was so special that the oil burned 8 nights. For more oil to be made? So the eternal light would keep on burning. Simplistic, don't you think? I think the real miracle was that our gift to the world never went out. Our tradition of being a light unto the nations, our desire to bring knowledge and justice and morality to the world (all another form of light), never flickered, much less died. The miracle is that we have always been able to share our light with others.

So when I teach my children about giving gifts, I ask them not to give what they think is cool, but to think about what the other person wants. And when my father refused to come into our house, he may have stood on his principles, but I think he missed the boat. He could have told me how important it was to him that our Judaism continue, and then he could have come inside, without compromising his own integrity while seeing how important it was to my then young, non-Jewish wife to be part of her family and ours.

Our gift of light and understanding. May it never go unkindled, and may this holiday season brighten the hearts of our global Jewish family.

Greetings From The Tooth Fairy

When my oldest son Ethan was 5 years old, he had it all figured out. "The tooth fairy," he told me, "sells the teeth she gets to the sandman. That's how she gets money to put under our pillows. The sandman grinds up the teeth and that's the sleep he puts in everyone's eyes."

Sure made sense to me. Every family has its own unique traditions. For many, lighting candles on Shabbat, blessing our children, and celebrating our holidays bind us together, not only as parents and children but as a people. Now I'm going to let you in on a little secret, if you promise not to tell my kids. In our family we have something special going on, because I AM THE TOOTH FAIRY!

It's not very Jewish. Or is it? Kids at the Hebrew Day School don't celebrate Halloween because…well, it's pagan. And I suppose the tooth fairy could be put in that category. Years ago I found a piece of clip art, colorized it, and now every time one of my children lose a tooth, they not only get a buck, they get a message from The Tooth Fairy.

I use it as an opportunity to teach, to say the words that might not be heard from Dad, but have a magical quality from their night visitor. My toothy muse inspires me to write more from my heart, to evoke messages of hope and prayer and longing and all the wishes I store up for my children that, when said aloud, are passed off as corny, uncomfortable, overblown. Fairy wisdom, however, passed on after midnight in exchange for bicuspids and molars, has a special power to capture attention and a place of honor in their hearts.

"Nothing's ever lost, it just changes hands, and in the changing, becomes more special because in some way the hands are joined in friendship."

"We learn responsibility with our adult teeth. We have to take care of them forever, and then they take care of us. Our big front teeth are our smiling teeth, the first thing people see when we open our mouth. Remember that when you brush your teeth, when you smile, and when you love. The love we grow lasts forever, too, as long as we take care of it with a smile in our hearts."

"It's all right to hold onto your dreams and wishes and fantasies for as long as you like. Dreams can't be taken away. They can only be dashed by people who can't imagine, by doubters who don't believe in the magic of love and the miracle of being alive. Make wishes. Hold onto your fantasies. Imagine all the what ifs in the world. And don't give up on me. Childhood doesn't last forever, and neither do your baby teeth. You'll be grown up soon enough. But for now, every day can be a mystery and a delight. Soak up each moment and dream, dream, dream."

"Losing your molars, your "big" baby teeth, is very symbolic. It means that you're passing from the games of childhood to "bigger" times and events. You're becoming more independent. You're thinking that your parents are always wrong (or maybe almost always), that they really don't know what's going on with you or understand you, that there are parts of yourself you keep deep inside, and other parts that are so exposed you feel like a raw nerve that's been stabbed by the world."

"Remember a few things when the weight of growing up gets to you. Remember you have friends and family who love you no matter what. Remember that it's all right to be nervous sometimes, afraid sometimes, and to still feel like a little kid sometimes. Remember that I love you, and your beautiful smile. And remember that fantasies and dreams are as real as you make them, and you make them real by making them come true, as you have made me come to life for you."

"Remember, your accomplishments will grow just like your permanent teeth, with deep roots, hidden layers of strength, and the power to bite through any obstacles that get in your way."

"Remember, a sweet smile brightens others' lives and is the doorway to a beautiful soul."

"When you lose your last tooth I will no longer be able to visit you. But remember, I will always be there with you, and you will always be in my heart. All you ever have to do is recall the best moments of your childhood, and hold my love and your parents' love close, and no matter how difficult the road may seem, how strange the times, how hard life may be, you will be all right, because you are wonderful, and those who know you best know this most of all.
Your friend, THE TOOTH FAIRY"

What's so Jewish about the Tooth Fairy? Nothing, really, and maybe everything. For in teaching lessons about love, loss, and the beauty of living, I am trying to make every day and the simplest things in life that we take for granted sacred to my children. And in that act, in my secret Tooth Fairy play, I transform the mundane into a miraculous world. I am The Tooth Fairy.

Children Of A Greater God

When you are growing up and someone asks you what you're the most scared of, the answer could be anything. Snakes. Spiders. Sharks. Thunder and lightning. The dark. But as you get older, if you have children there is only one answer to the question. Losing a child is the greatest fear of all.

Judaism is filled with stories about the death of children. Cain kills Abel. And the Jewish conscience is born. Are we our brothers and sisters keepers? Yes. A thousand times yes. God spares Isaac, and faith and mercy and commitment become tenets of our faith. Pharaoh slays the first born, but Moses is saved and goes on to be our greatest leader. The first born of Egypt are slain, and amidst the horror the Jewish people are freed. How many of our beliefs is founded on the fear of losing a child, and the lessons of hope and mercy and redemption? I daresay more than we suspect.

Some years ago friends of ours had a child diagnosed with cancer. One night, as my wife and I were going to Orlando Regional Hospital for a parenting class, we ran into them coming out of a cancer support group. Their daughter had lost all her hair at this point in her treatments, and in solidarity and love, both parents shaved their heads to match hers. I learned more going into that class about love and commitment than I ever did walking out. And I believe that the close bonds of a Jewish family and the support of friends and their faith and resolute love helped see them through. Their daughter is fine. So are they. And I am a better father because of them.

I am the father of three, and as a father I dream of life affirming events in some distant future – bar and bat mitzvot, the anxiety of separation when my children move away, marriages and grandchildren and God knows what else. I imagine congratulating them in their successes in life, and commiserating with them over their failures. I see Ethan playing baseball, and Jerica teaching college, and Gabriel, with the whole world at his feet. But I can't see a world without them, and when something bad does happen, as it inevitably will, I thank God and fate and the powers of the universe that it's only a broken leg, the flu, that they're home safe in bed and tomorrow they'll be safe as well.

And then tonight I get an e-mail, the night after the most recent bombing in Israel, when a homicide bomber blew up a bus loaded with students, and a nine-year old girl is killed and most of the bodies have not yet been identified. We have friends who live in Jerusalem and I think of them immediately. The e-mail, written by the friends of local residents, is haunting, sad, and recounts, in part, the death of a husband and his pregnant wife in a murderous attack on a mobile home in Karmei Tzur. And I imagine the sheer audacity and bravery of parenting in Israel, when every time you put your child on a bus you say a prayer. When every time your child goes to a fast food restaurant with friends you listen fearfully for sirens. When every time you go out for a family picnic or a vacation at the beach you watch your back. I cannot, honestly, imagine the strength of conviction these brave, audacious people must have. I, who cry at the distant thought of an imagined calamity to one of my children, and they live it every day.

Is there a message here? Yes, albeit an indirect one. First, a gift to the Israel Emergency Campaign will buy security for Israeli schoolchildren and bulletproof buses and counseling for the bereaved. And second, thank God for our people, whose children will never strap bombs to their bodies, who will never be praised for taking a life, whose greatest fear is losing a child. In our fear of loss we affirm our love of life. In our love of life we shout our commitment to tomorrow. We are the brave, the audacious, the resolute, hope filled children of Israel. We are children of God.

David Bornstein

2003

Baseball Dawn

Bar Mitzvah Blues

Ethan has done it again. Pinned on his bedroom wall, between baseball trophy plaques, is a page torn out of Sports Illustrated. The picture's one of baseball's most moving moments, when Lou Gehrig gave his farewell speech. The headline above the picture reads, "To some it's a sport. To others, a religion." When he hung it up he pointed it out to me proudly. "See?" he said. "That's me." My eyebrows curled. I thought for a moment about an appropriate response, holding my knee jerk "Judaism is your religion" in check. I knew, at that moment, it would do no good. So I smiled, bookmarked the scene, and said, "I know how important baseball is to you. Have you done your bar mitzvah study yet?"

With a boy like Ethan it's easy to lose perspective. You see, having a baseball player wasn't even on the list of predictions for our children. I could have imagined author, musician, computer geek, punk skateboarder, even tennis player, but southpaw pitcher? I don't think so. It's one thing to have a kid who enjoys sports or plays what we condescendingly call "rec ball," or little league. It's another to support a child with scholarship potential. When you have a child who excels in any area, and who makes a willing commitment to it, as a parent your job becomes helping them reach their potential.

Ethan has made that commitment. His standard week includes a team practice, a doubleheader, a pitching lesson, a strength and conditioning workout, batting cages, long toss, soft toss, throwing weighted balls and fielding drills. Our lives seem to revolve around the stitches of a baseball. Where, then, does religious education fit in?

To be honest, this year had been a struggle. Hebrew school conflicts with baseball practice, Sunday school with games. We've balanced that reasonably well, but it's still easy to get a skewed viewpoint. That all changed as we thought about the real meaning of his bar mitzvah.

At a b'nai mitzvah meeting at our shul, the rabbi, education director and cantor all made it clear in the most positive way that the lessons our children must recall are about the responsibilities that come with transitioning into a Jewish adult, not recounting their first words, diaper training or home runs. So first, we have to remember that we're sharing the experience with our synagogue. It's part of a religious service, not merely a family celebration. That may seem obvious, but when I've imagined talking to Ethan on the bimah, what's always come to mind are his exploits on the field, not in the field of study.

What I realized, what I've begun to speak to Ethan about, and what is particularly difficult to convey to a twelve or thirteen year old, is that who they are today is just today. Many things change in life – friends, athletic abilities, homes, schools – but one constant is an internal identity, a communal consciousness and religious base that Judaism can provide. For the teen who retains a sense of restless immortality, the belief that life is long and today is everything, it's hard to inculcate an understanding that life is both long and fleeting, that we must make the most of our moments and the most of our years, that who we are is defined by how we live and what we believe as well as what we accomplish. Those three areas form the foundation of my own Jewish sensibilities. And that is what I've tried to impart to my oldest son, for years by example, for the months leading up to his bar mitzvah.

In his farewell speech Lou Gehrig said, "I may have had a tough break, but I have an awful lot to live for." In my short speech to my son, already spinning in my head, I won't talk about baseball, but I may talk about Torah. I won't talk about fame, but I may mention faith. As individuals our flames are bright. As Jews they're eternal. We have so much to live for. I only hope that through the bar mitzvah experience I convey that idea to my son. Life is full of tough breaks, but the toughest of all would be missing the rare opportunity to be a committed Jew.

To My Son
On The Eve Of His Bar Mitzvah

Dear Ethan,

I've held onto some of the thoughts I'm putting down for 13 years. Just thinking about your bar mitzvah, I feel the floodgates open, and I am awash in messages I want to convey to you.

First (and I believe you already know this), I am very proud of you, and hope you are equally proud of yourself. You've grown quickly into a young man, a wonderful teenage combination of intelligence and goofiness, seriousness and comic relief, compassion and rage. I admire all your extremes, the intense way you attack and absorb the world. You have balanced commitments to your Judaism, your family, and your extracurricular activities without sacrificing who you are. Core to you, I'm convinced, are your Jewish roots.

A bar mitzvah is a coming of age. That doesn't mean you are "of age" yet. It means that our sages and teachers, many years ago in their deepest wisdom, recognized, as cultures have recognized for millennia, that this transitional time is truly a turning point in life. Growing up is hard. Your emotions and hormones will continue to go crazy for a while. You'll feel like a little boy who needs a hug one second, a self-assured man who can't imagine asking for help the next. The only advice I can give you there is that it's always all right to ask for help and a hug. We need them both, for people don't exist in a vacuum and can't make it alone forever.

Choices you make from here on out will have great consequence, not on who you become, for you will always be in a state of becoming, but on how well you travel the road of becoming. Drugs, sex, following the wrong crowd or making the right call – it's more up to you now than ever before.

Life doesn't get any easier. You'll move from worrying about your friends to your girlfriends to someday, if it's meant to be, your family and children. Let me tell you, concern for your spouse and children feels more like a tidal wave of responsibility than anything you will ever face in life, and with it comes levels of joy and astonishment, growth and change unlike anything else you will ever experience. I have learned more from watching you grow up, from being your dad and your friend and your teacher and your coach and yes, sometimes your pain in the butt dictator, than all my years of schooling combined. I know you will be up to the task of adulthood. I also know where you can go for help when your family's not quite big enough – your extended family, your Jewish community.

You see, it wasn't that long ago that I ran from my community. In college I avoided saying my last name because it sounded so Jewish. I never went to services, never visited Hillel. I explored alternative religions and the counterculture of the 70's in an attempt to figure out who I was and who I wasn't. Then an amazing thing happened. Your grandparents gently, casually, steered me back.

Perhaps it was the deep sense of familiarity, warmth and security of reciting the prayers at High Holy Day services. Perhaps it was looking around the synagogue and realizing that this was my home base, where my support structures and power lunches were. Perhaps it was making friends and building alliances through community volunteer work. Perhaps it was the recognition of being part of a people who have been and still are a light unto the nations. Really, it was all the above that made me realize I had more going for me and more help behind me than I had ever dreamed as I grew up. Now, looking back in my middle age, with children who are growing up, I understand that you may not fully accept this now, but I hope you do someday.

So my wishes for you are simple, imbued with my love, my admiration, and my lifetime commitment to you. Be kind to yourself and others. Cut yourself some slack. Be patient. The world gets rougher as you get older. Look to your family, your Jewish community, and your Jewish traditions and teachings for strength and support. It's all there if you only ask for it. And it's all in the blessing below that parents and rabbis have recited for generations.

Y'va-reh'ha Adonai v'yish-m-reha. May the Lord bless you and protect you. Ya-eyr Adonai panav eyle-ha vi-huneka. May the Lord show you kindness and be gracious to you. Yisa Adonai panav ehle-ha v'ya-seym l'ha shalom. May the Lord bestow favor upon you and grant you peace. Amen.

Faith

A few weeks ago my son Ethan and I took a trip to San Antonio to visit David and Joanne S. David is a long time friend from high school, and our last night there Joanne asked me a simple question that has reverberated deep inside me ever since. "Do you ever question your faith?" It seems she was. They are Catholic, and a Vietnamese priest had been installed in their church. They couldn't understand him and felt like they were losing touch with their Sunday services and their religion.

What they were losing wasn't their faith, really. It was their connection. But when Joanne asked me, and I attempted an answer, a Pandora's box of questions imploded inside me.

You see, I have had numerous reasons to question my faith recently. I haven't doubted my commitment to my Judaism, but I have been asking a lot of questions, about my faith in myself, my faith in others, and in some ways, my faith in the Torah, in the word of God.

My questions have come about because of a confluence of incidents. Joanne's question was the icing the cake, if you will. I have, for many months, had running dialogues with my brother who is, in his own right, a deeply spiritual man with a strong commitment to personal growth. I regularly send him commentary on the Torah, and from time to time he takes offense at the weekly portion. Perhaps it speaks of a vengeful, judgmental God. Perhaps it is about the Jewish people's conquest of the promised land. Perhaps it sounds anti-woman, or anti-gay. Whatever the reason, he has asked how I can appreciate a religion that year in and year out reads material that is violent, harsh, and negative, while he searches for a religion that promotes peace, understanding, hope, and faith in the goodness of the universe. He reads books like "Conversations with God," and seeks a purity of purpose and morality, a sensibility that rarely exists in this convoluted world. And while I don't believe that the level of purity he aspires to exists, I have looked at the Biblical passages he refers to with disdain, and I, too, often find myself disliking them.

On top of that, this has been a particularly tough baseball season for Ethan, not because he has done poorly. In fact, statistically he's had the best season of his life. It's because he's had a coach who, for the first time ever, didn't have faith in him. I have found myself becoming overly protective, suffering more than Ethan as I tended to his wounded self-esteem. I have questioned my faith in others, in the authority figures and coaches I rely on to help guide my children, as I have watched them play favorites, criticize without thinking to praise. And I've worried that perhaps a personality conflict between myself and this coach has hurt my son. Perhaps it's my fault. Perhaps I'm to blame. I've begun the painful process of stripping away some of my bravado, my masks of certainty, my egotism wrapped around my ability to make things right, and my questions have multiplied. Why does someone form opinions about someone else and refuse to change them? Why are people unfair? Why do people with power and influence abuse their power and hurt the innocent? Why can't we be good?

So where is my faith? What do I want to believe?

I believe that faith is internal and eternal, that it comes from within and while it may be dinged and damaged from without, survives despite questions, uncertainty, and doubt.

I have faith in others, because of the strength of family, the support of community. In the hardest times I have received help and nurturance from the most surprising places.

I have faith in myself as I learn to have compassion for myself and forgive myself. I trust that my intentions are good, regardless of my constantly questioning everything around me, including me.

I have faith that redemption is possible, that babies are born innocent, that while people may be stuck in a quagmire of moral dilemmas, there is always something good to be found.

I have faith that a world of grays and inconclusive endings is all right. My faith is flexible, malleable, interpretive and evolutionary. Judaism isn't about heaven or hell, either/or, yes/no. We find truth in grains of sand, then reinterpret the sand and find other meanings. We are not absolute. We are radically philosophical and fanatically open. We question. We doubt. We hope. And sometimes we despair. But not forever. Faith doesn't work like that. It's transformative, and because it transforms, it is timeless as it begs us to ask the difficult questions: Who am I? Why am I? Where am I going?

Years ago my sister made an inspirational collage out of photographs, comic books and magazine headlines. I still have it hanging in my office. Two quotes stand out. The first is anonymous: "My faith in me is stronger than all your armies, governments, gas chambers...," The second was written by Jorge Luis Borges. It has become my personal mantra, the first step in my quest for faith: "I reach my center, my algebra and my key, my mirror. Soon I shall know who I am."

David Bornstein

Mourn The Columbia

Our community just concluded a memorial ceremony for the Columbia astronauts, including, of course, Ilan Ramon, the Israeli pilot, hero, and crew member who died aboard the shuttle. I didn't attend, not out of disrespect or disregard for the event, but simply because, when I asked a simple question, I came up with no good answer: Why are we having this service? And when I asked the question, I decided to stay home with my wife and children and write my answer.

As is often the case, the question begged other questions. Were we mourning because a Jew was on board? Would we have held the ceremony if he wasn't? What did we do as a community when the Challenger exploded (honestly I don't recall)? Why don't we mourn at a public ceremony whenever a terrorist attack kills tens of Israelis? Why don't we cry when a commercial plane goes down, killing hundreds? Does it matter if a disaster occurs over the skies of the United States, Israel, or Indonesia? What is the difference between seven people dying in a space shuttle and seven people dying from cancer, or a terrorist bomb, or a car accident or tornado? Every day the Orlando obits have more than seven names. Maybe the answer is there's no difference at all.

Let's face facts. There were only seven people aboard the Columbia. Each of them volunteered for something that, while superficially routine, is in actuality a bullet slung on a bomb into outer space and returned to land through 3,000° heat. The real differences are media and technology related. The heart wrenching disaster made great headlines. The shuttle, loaded with links to schools and children's experiments, with a wonderfully multiracial, multi-religious, global crew was a snapshot of the new America, and because of that touched many of us (though truth be told, when a plane crashes we could probably say the same). So first, callous as it sounds, our ceremony was media created.

Second, something occurs to our psyches when the routine and mundane (a shuttle mission) suddenly goes awry. The ground feels unsteady, as if we stand in the midst of an earthquake. Our faith quakes as well. Technological wonders, on which we base so much of our hope for the future, no longer seem wondrous. They become fragile, complex to a fault, compromised by slashed budgets and shallow scrutiny. And so our sense of our own well being, our secure world comes into question, and we feel queasy and unsettled, as if everything we take for granted should now be questioned. And the truth is that questions are good, but good goes wrong, and even the most redundant systems can fail. As Jews we have prayers for almost everything, not to trivialize, but to appreciate the smallest aspects of the miracle of life. Life is fragile and delicate, so perhaps the answer here is to live each day taking nothing for granted. Then, when the mundane turns macabre, we may be shaken, but our faith in the beauty of existence won't break.

Finally, I can only hope that our public ceremony didn't occur solely because Ilan Ramon was on board. I do believe that the only people who will take care of Jews are Jews. I believe that we are a special, unique people, with great gifts that have benefited humanity. I also believe we are only people, no more or less than anyone else, and thus should never be exalted above others. We can take pride in our heritage and traditions without placing our heroes on pedestals. All life is essentially sacred, and so, in my mind, there is no quantitative distinction between a life lost on a life raft between Cuba and Florida or a space craft 40 miles above Texas. Both are tragic. Both may contain heroes. Both deserve our prayers and acknowledgement.

I mourn for Israel's loss, at a time when she so desperately needs heroes. I mourn for NASA, for I believe that space exploration is a great adventure that will continue to benefit humankind. I mourn for the families of the seven astronauts lost to a terrible accident, and I mourn for America, which now questions itself once again. And as I mourn I value every life lost, every birth, every death, every day that gives us all life, hope, and breath.

2004

Stained Glass

The Shallow Pond

Zell Kravinsky, we would all agree, is a unique, no, an odd man. An article in The New Yorker (Aug. 2, 2004) tells how Kravinsky, a Ph.D. in composition theory, a math whiz, and a self-made millionaire in real estate by age 45, gave away his entire $45 million estate to charity. Kravinsky donated most of his fortune to the Centers for Disease Control Foundation and the Ohio State University School of Public Health.

Then he went a step further. "In the months following the first of Kravinsky's financial gifts, a new ratio began to preoccupy him: the one-in-four thousand chance that a person has of dying in an operation to donate a kidney." He decided, against the wishes of his wife, children, and close friends, to make a "non-directed" donation of one of his kidneys. Only 134 similar donations have been made in the United States - giving a kidney, where the demand far outstrips the supply, to someone the donor doesn't know. Kravinsky went through with the donation, giving his kidney to a 29-year-old single black woman studying for a degree in social work, who had been on dialysis for eight years.

Kravinsky's acts of uncompromising, extremist altruism go farther than almost any rational philanthropist would go. But his life and his choices, when analyzed seriously, force us to ask the most difficult, basic questions about charity. What is a life worth? Is it morally wrong not to give away money (or other requirements for life) that you don't need to provide the most basic necessities for others? Kravinsky was asked to calculate a ratio between his love for his children and his compassion for unknown children. "I don't know where I'd set it," he answered, "but I would not let many children die so my kids could live. I don't think that two kids should die so that one of my kids has comfort, and I don't know that two children should die so that one of my kids lives."

Parenting and the unequivocal defense response we feel towards our own children aside, Kravinsky has a point. When is one life of luxury worth more than two, whether they're other wealthy children, living in abject poverty or simply no names in a distant land?

In a famous 1972 essay, the Australian philosopher Peter Singer established the ethical puzzle now known as the Shallow Pond and the Envelope. In the first situation, Singer sees a child drowning in a shallow pond. He considers saving the child, and reflects on the inconvenience of muddying his clothes. In the second he receives a letter from the Bengal Relief Fund asking him to send a donation overseas to save childrens' lives.

If he ignores the drowning child, we consider his decision immoral and inhumane. (We even have a similar situation that occurred in our own community, when Jason Toll heroically saved a drowning child without considering his own safety.) If he throws the envelope away, we understand his response (and the law supports this position). Singer contends that the two scenarios are ethically alike. "If we can prevent something bad without sacrificing anything of comparable significance, we ought to do it," he writes.

Others disagree. Colin McGinn, a philosopher at Rutgers, calls Singer's principle "positively bad," for it "encourages a way of life in which many important values are sacrificed to generalized altruism. Just think of how much the human race would have lost if Newton and Darwin and Leonardo and Socrates had spent their time on charitable acts!"

This is the foundation upon which Jewish charity is built, and the question Federations across the United States ask each year as they fund raise in tough times. If our agencies and local needs are, at least metaphorically, drowning children, and overseas needs are envelopes we receive in the mail, how do you give the envelope the same moral weight as the drowning child? It's too easy to say no when a solicitor talks about starving Jews in Ethiopia. It's too easy to not care about elderly Jews in Russia. They're nameless, faceless, far away. But they exist nonetheless. They're people in need, and what's more, they're Jews. Put a picture on the envelope. Give the face a name, and it still doesn't resonate to thousands of Jews here in Central Florida who don't give a dime. But ask them to give books to their child's nursery school, or pay for a class outing, or blow a wad on a birthday party, and they ante up like the New York Yankees with free agents. The goal, somehow, must be to get the message across that the lives of millions around the world are as meaningful as the lives of the few of us here. One for one, we're all important, but in the shallow pond of Jewish survival, when comparing the one to the many, we have to figure out a way to make charity for the many as valued as saving a child next door.

Humanity In The Face Of Horror

I did something foolish and horrible last week. I downloaded and watched the video of the beheading/execution of Nicholas Berg. At first it was like a glorified lynching, reminiscent of the KKK as the hooded terrorists read something in Arabic, with Berg on his knees in front of them. Then it got grisly. The worst part of the low quality tape was the screaming, the painful, gut–wrenching screams of a man having his throat cut, his head severed while he was still alive. My skin crawled; my stomach turned. I felt like throwing up as the blood pooled under poor, innocent Nicholas Berg. I won't tell you I had nightmares about the scene. I didn't. I think, instead, that I've blocked it from my mind. But I can tell you I'm scared that, as my rabbi said in a recent sermon, we're dealing with monsters here, and monsters are the inhabitants of our worst nightmares.

What has troubled me in the face of the Berg murder is the seeming knee jerk need to compare the atrocity to the different but atrocious humiliations and tortures that took place at Abu Ghraib Prison. I agree with those who say that the abuse of Iraqi prisoners was used as an excuse for the beheading, not a rationale for it. I agree with those who say comparing prisoner abuse to murder is an apples to oranges deal, that people can recover from abuse, while death is irreversible. I agree with those who equate the beheading to the death of Daniel Pearl, another innocent Jew murdered because their sin was…they were in the wrong place at the wrong time? They were naïve in thinking they were safe? They were Jewish?

I don't agree with anyone who tries to negate the horrors of Abu Ghraib by comparing them to the beheading of Nicholas Berg. In the May 17 issue of The New Yorker, columnist David Remnick writes, "From the beginning of the war in Iraq, the Administration's rhetoric placed moral progress at the heart of its mission. "I call on all governments to join with the United States and the community of law-abiding nations in prohibiting, investigating, and prosecuting all acts of torture, "President Bush said last June, emphasizing the ethical underpinnings of Operation Iraqi Freedom. "We are leading this fight by example." The sentiment was laudable – and it is precisely what has made the revelations of American misconduct in Abu Ghraib so profoundly disheartening."

As Jews we are the world's greatest example of a people dedicated to law and codes of morality. We established the underpinnings of ethical behavior, from the Ten Commandments to Hillel's original Golden Rule: "Do not unto others as you would have others do not unto you." We have been asked to carry the heavy burden of conscience and morality in a world that defies reason. At the same time, we have evolved from a people who were slaughtered by Nazis and fought back in pockets of resistance to a people who are defiantly proud and will not be driven into the sea, no matter the odds against us.

We are dealing with monsters - irrational, ugly, frightening monsters who I, unfortunately, believe must be eradicated from the face of the earth because there is no solution they will accept other than the destruction of world Jewry, Christianity, and democracy. But I don't want us to lose our humanity in the process. At Abu Ghraib Muslim prisoners were forced into abject humiliation, made to act out male-to-male sex acts, to pile naked on one another in stark contrast to the tenets of their faith. Torture scars for life, and there is no rationale, no reason a moral country should stoop so low. Let's not lose sight of who we are, lest we begin to tread the paths of the monsters we seek to destroy, both in our psyches and in the real world. And when we find the real monsters out there, the ones who kill shamelessly, who target the innocent and have neither regret nor remorse, let's surgically, precisely, deftly remove them from the living as quickly as possible.

Did You Bring Me Anything?

This is as much a column about Chanukah last year as it is Chanukah this year. You see, we're still in recovery mode 12 months later. Last year Gabriel was three and just old enough to grasp the full impact of eight nights of gifts in a row. Unfortunately, he wasn't old enough to understand that after eight nights the gifts were supposed to stop. Something happened in his quick little brain, and the repeated pattern of candle lighting and gift giving (whether small or large) coupled with our natural inclination to spoil our last baby turned him into a "what have you done for me lately" monster. We're still paying for it. Every time I come home, whether I've been gone all day or for just twenty minutes to buy some milk, when I walk in the door Gabriel asks, "Did you bring me anything?"

My answers have undergone numerous transformations. They started with the simple, "No I didn't" and evolved to "Yes I did. I brought you ME!" He didn't buy it. I told him I brought him my love. His answer was he already knew that. I told him to stop asking for presents or he wouldn't get anything, but that didn't matter since I wasn't bringing toys home every time I stepped out anyway. So he'd stop asking for a little while, and then start up again.

I threatened. I cajoled. I joked. I'd bring home the occasional cheap toy or educational tool – a book, art supplies – I'd even make my older son get a happy meal from McDonald's so I could give Gabriel the toy. But all I did was make the problem worse, not better, and the warped spirit of Chanukah giving lasted throughout the year.

Now we're coming full circle, back to a minor holiday I've learned to love and dread. Like any rational Jewish parents we toyed with and quickly dismissed the idea of no gift giving. The combined burdens of Christmas competition and unadulterated love make the idea of holidays without presents almost inconceivable. What's a parent to do?

Some answers that come to mind are obvious. We can use the old standby of a big gift the first and last night and small gifts in between. We can remind our children that part of the reason they get gifts is so they don't feel insignificant relative to our Christian neighbors' orgy of Christmas gift giving, but doesn't that teach them to be grateful for Christmas? We can focus on the fun part of the holiday – the latkes and dreidels and the beauty of the chanukiah – but that seems to be misdirection rather than explanation.

So here are the two things I'm going to try to convey to my four year old this year. First, I'll teach the lessons of Chanukah and hope that over time everything else will fall into place. Remember that while the holiday celebrates a victory in war, it commemorates a holy miracle, and our Jewish gratitude for the miracle of eight days and nights of light that symbolized our neverending connection to God, should never be forgotten or diminished.

Second, I'll emphasize that a large part of the joy of Chanukah is celebrating family. From the Brother Maccabees who won a war to Jewish families today lighting candles for eight nights, Chanukah is about sharing and being together. It's about remembering the miracle of love and reflecting on the miracle of light. It's about being conscious of our Jewish role in the world, of what makes us different, unique, and special. It's about the beauty of survival and the joy of giving as well as receiving.

Gabriel was the only child in his class this year who, when asked what he was thankful for during Thanksgiving, answered, "God." I think this year I'll fret less about the effect of giving gifts eight nights in a row, and focus more on the underlying message of Chanukah. If I do, I believe my children will respond with Jewish hearts and souls that appreciate the miracles of light, life, love, and a relationship with God.

Age

Gabriel, my four year old, woke up and got himself a glass of water tonight. I happened to be unable to sleep myself, so I met him when he walked down the stairs, a thirsty little boy scared of a bad dream. I picked him up, told him he could always call for Mommy or Daddy if he needed us in the middle of the night, and took him to sleep in our bed.

None of this is such a big deal, except Gabriel got himself a glass of water. No longer a baby, he's growing up in a big way. So are my other children. When I talk with Jerica I realize she's responding in surprisingly sophisticated ways, and I'm left wondering how she suddenly got so mature. And whenever we take Ethan out with us now he's getting hit on by teenage girls.

This all occurs to me after a week of reflection on my own age. A friend and business associate, upon hearing that I would soon be turning 48, remarked "You're getting to be an old man!" Not old yet, but I'm certainly not a kid anymore.

And then I took a drive to look at property in Polk and Lake counties. I passed Polo Park, the huge community my father and I developed, and I drove north into Clermont and saw how the orange groves I'd played in as a child had been stripped and razed to make way for new housing developments, and the traffic on those country roads had increased dramatically since the days I picked oranges with my brother and father, and sadly, as a developer I am partly the cause of my memories' alterations, as the hills make way for houses.

I'm not old, not yet, but I'm feeling my age without the mid life crisis of a forty year old, without the wise acceptance of an octogenarian, but rather with wistfulness and wonder tinged with questions and regret. What if I'd made other choices?

What if I'd followed a different path years ago, when the road ahead wasn't nearly so well defined?

"Teach us to number our days rightly, that we obtain a wise heart," the Psalms (90:11) teach us. Dylan Thomas, the great Irish poet, took a contrary stance. "Do not go gentle into that good night," he wrote. "Rage, rage against the dying of the light." But as Jews, without an emphasis on the afterlife, what are we to hang onto, to grasp as we see twilight approaching? The few biblical portraits we have of the elderly portray men less well than women in their waning years. Rebecca keeps her family together with her spirit and strength until the end of her life. Moses, it's true, is blessed till the last with undiminished vision and vigor. But none of our other male role models come off so well. Neither Isaac nor David is a model of vigor and wisdom in his old age. In the end, a hapless and helpless King David does manage to redeem himself with one touching truth as he speaks with acceptance of his passing to his son Solomon, "I am going the way of all the earth; be strong and show yourself a man (I Kings 2:2)."

The difference in handling the adversity of old age may have as much to do with how men and women spend their younger years as with biology. Meaning for men comes too often from their role in public venues where they labor to provide for their families and struggle to affect the space in which they work. When the workplace ceases to be central, there is risk of a decline in personal meaning and self-esteem.

So I sit here, late at night in front of my computer screen, listening to Gabriel shift restlessly in our bed, wondering what I'll be like when my work days and volunteer days are over, when my children have left and Pat and I are once again, a couple alone with each other, alone with ourselves. I find that I'm at odds with myself, grateful for the direction of my life, the blessings of my wife and children, and yet beginning to feel a slow burn against the imperfections, the losses and failures that are inevitable in every life. I am caught with feet in two worlds, one of acceptance and contentment, one of rage as I battle against the fading light.

Perhaps this is where Judaism is wise beyond words, in the deepest, most heartfelt ways, for the emphasis of our faith is on caring for each other, reflected in the words we recite in Hebrew each time we finish reading a book of the Torah, completing, as it were, another cycle of study and reflection: "Be strong, be strong and let us strengthen each other." By sharing our lives, our needs, our frailties and strengths we have the ability to realize our potential in our old age, by becoming a source of meaning and wisdom for our children, our friends, and our communities.

Life Without Judaism

My children are my greatest teachers. Every so often incidents converge, and they dunk me into a deep pool of introspection, self-reflection, and epiphanies. This past weekend was that kind of time.

First, my four year old Gabriel showed me the yoga poses he learned from his pregnant Israeli teacher at the Jewish Community Center. The warrior pose. The triangle. The child pose. He moved through them flawlessly, flowing as if made for the movements. Yoga at the JCC. I like the contrast and the fact that a synthesis of philosophies could take place without interfering with his budding Jewish identity.

Then, my ten year old daughter Jerica had her horseback riding lesson rained out on Sunday morning. Jerica goes horseback riding three times a week. Her skills are growing rapidly, and now she's cantering and jumping with ease. She was ready to ride her bike to Apopka (20 miles from home) to make her lesson. What commitment, I thought. What passion for something she loves.

Finally, Ethan had an innocent conversation with other boys on his baseball team about the word Jew. I didn't intervene but I listened closely. "Would you be offended if we called you a Jew?" they asked. "No," Ethan replied, "but it depends on how you say it. If you say "he's a Jew" it can be ok or bad. But you can say he's Jewish and it's ok. And calling someone a dirty Jew is really bad." And on the way to Sunday school, after a half hour of not wanting to go that melted into resignation, Ethan asked me what his life would be like if he weren't Jewish. "I wouldn't have all the money I got from my bar mitzvah," he said.

'You wouldn't have a sense of who you are," I replied.

"Sure I would," he said. "I'd just believe that Jesus is the son of G-d and that he could take away all my sins."

"You know I don't believe that," I said.

"Neither do I," he answered.

But on the drive home through the rain I couldn't stop thinking, "I didn't give a good answer." What would my life be like if I weren't Jewish? What would be different? I'd still have a community around me. It would just be a different community, say, a Christian one instead of a Jewish one. I'd still have a set of beliefs grounded in ancient text and discourse. I would still believe in the ten commandments, in education, in doing good for the less fortunate. If I were Catholic I'd still retain a strong sense of guilt as an undeniable part of my culture. If I were Buddhist I'd focus on the moment, comparable in some ways to a universally present, all-knowing G-d.

As Jews we don't focus on the hereafter, on karma, on reincarnation or heaven and hell. We believe, in the core of our beings, that our actions today count for everything, not because of what they will bring us somewhere down the line (a spot in heaven, a more evolved body the next time around), but because of what we can change now. We believe in living right and doing good so the world can improve as a whole, not so we can be better off as individuals. That is an enormous, singular difference.

And I have to believe that the bonds I feel for my fellow Jews, the fact that when I struggle, when I doubt, when I need, I turn to my (Jewish) friends, I rely on my (Jewish) community. I believe I can "go to the Jewish well" of camaraderie and commiseration and drink deeply without being weighed down by unconscionable debt. I believe that we have added something beneficial, intelligent and beautiful and mystical to the world, and that those contributions ought to continue. I believe that Louis Brandeis and Albert Einstein and Bob Dylan and millions of other brilliant minds and artists and humanitarians would not have existed and contributed to the reshaping of our miraculous world were it not for their being Jewish. I believe in making today as much as I can because I am a Jew, not for myself alone but for us all together. That's the message, or at least the beginning of one, that I want to convey to my children. As they ask the fundamental question of adulthood: "Who am I?" I want them to know that a central part of the answer is that they are Jews.

2005

Candles In Jerusalem

The Value Of Generations

I'm focused on the challenge of bringing Judaism into a hectic modern household, and lo and behold, I just realized I'm sitting on examples of how others brought Judaism to me. So this is a tale of two generations separated by nearly a century: my grandfather, Ed Peisner, who died more than 25 years ago at age 90, and my five year old son Gabriel.

My Grampa Ed was a classic local character, well known and well loved by many early Jewish Orlandoans for his warmth and sense of humor. He was the chazzan at Temple Israel for years, coming as he did from a long line of Russian rabbis. Once, when he was very old, almost completely deaf and blind, he was walking around the block for exercise when Sam Behr drove by. In his southern drawl, Sam said, "Mr. Peisner, you know who this is?" Without seeing him clearly, my grandfather stopped and replied, "Eet can't be a lion, and eet isn't a tiger, so it must surely be a bear."

My parents invited him to live with us when I was 6 years old, shortly after my grandmother died. Years later he told us that their offer probably saved his life, but I think in many ways he saved ours, though this was an understanding I didn't come to for many years.

People used to walk up to me and tell me how wonderful and patient I was to have my grandfather living with us, and I'd nod my head and say it wasn't a big deal. But the truth was, I wasn't patient. He was an embarrassment to me. Once on New Years Eve, when my parents were out at a party I was setting off firecrackers and he came outside in his pajamas without his teeth in, yelling "Bang! Bang! Vhat's all dhat noise!" To my shame I ignored him and continued setting off cherry bombs. And another time when my parents were out of town and I had a few hundred of my closest high school friends I'd never met over for a party, he told me I was "destroying my parents' faith in me," and then locked himself in his room. Maybe not theirs, but his for sure. He always led us in the Shabbat blessings on Friday nights, and even though my brother and I often didn't take him or his commitment to Shabbat very seriously, it was because of him that Friday nights were always a little different, a little more special in our house.

But now, you see, I've come full circle. I'm the one who starts the blessings for my family on Shabbat, and I wonder if my children take me seriously. And then I look at Gabriel, who loves Shabbat and has a kosher soul. Let me clarify that. At age 3 Gabriel started talking about wanting to be a vegetarian so he wouldn't hurt animals, and my wife proceeded to explain kashrut to him, and how Jews believe in killing animals as painlessly as possible, at which point he decided he would only eat kosher meat.

This morning we made turkey sausages for breakfast for our kids. Gabriel asked his mother if they were kosher. I looked on the package, and as much as I wanted him to have some protein, I couldn't find the kosher symbol and couldn't lie to him, so I said, "No, Gabriel, they're turkey sausage, so it's not beef, but they're not kosher." And he wouldn't eat them. Then he asked me if I wanted to start eating kosher meat like he was, and I said yes I do. "That's good, Daddy," he replied. "You and I will make God proud."

What do you say to that? Absolutely nothing, because his innate child's wisdom eclipsed my clumsy adult intent.

And this is what I've realized. Sometimes it's not what I bring into the house that makes our lives Jewish. It's what those I love bring me that makes me Jewish. When I recall my grandfather now, I'm embarrassed at myself for my impatience and laughter, but look what he gave me: blessings on Shabbat, a sensitivity to the needs of the elderly, and a reflection, years later, of myself and what I want to give my children. And from

Gabriel I see that Judaism sometimes can't be taught. It has to be felt on the deepest levels. The greatest lessons I've learned about being Jewish have come to me through the years and despite the years, from past to present, from the oldest and youngest of my family, and I'm grateful for both.

Eulogy For Ella

A woman I've known almost my entire life died this past week. Her name didn't make it into any splashy local obituary, maybe because she was poor, or black, or didn't do anything more earthshaking in her life than raise her own children, grandchildren, and a family of Jewish children – me, my sister and brother.

Her name was Ella Mae Sullivan, and this is a short tribute to a hard life lived with heart.

Some of you may have met her, and others may have known someone just like her. I don't know if it was a southern phenomenon, or a southern Jewish one, to have a fat, black woman cook, keep house and care for kids during the 50's and 60's. She came in around 10 a.m. and left after dinner, which started promptly at 6 p.m. every night Monday through Friday, with Ella leaning on her elbows by the stove and watching us, waiting until we were done and there were dishes to load and leftovers to put away. The house was never perfectly clean, and the vegetables were always overcooked, but it didn't matter, because she was a fixture in our lives as much as anyone. She was family.

Over the years Ella became my idea of an ideal mother, one who gives love unconditionally, without judgment or disappointment or impossible standards to live up to. It's not that our parents aren't good and loving, but the parent-child relationship is inherently loaded with the baggage of expectation and the fear of separation. There was none of that with Ella. It was pure love, and when she wrapped her arms around me, I knew I was enveloped in a warm, all-encompassing embrace.

I'll never forget Shabbats with Ella. After so many years with my family, she could Baruch Ata Adonai with the best of us. She had a special relationship with my grandfather, Ed Peisner, who lived with us from the time I was six years old. She'd cook his favorite foods and take his best (and worst) jokes without ever getting upset. "Oh, Mr. Peisner, you crack me up," she said a dozen times a day.

I'll never forget my brother's bar mitzvah. It wasn't enough that my sister's hippie boyfriend came in sandals, or that her best friends wore dashikis and beads, or that I had long hair and wore a brown velour suit. When Ella walked in and sat in the back I insisted she come up front and sit with us. She was wearing gigantic, gaudy costume jewelry – beads and sequins and fake furs, and when my family traipsed down the aisle after services she walked with us, waving and smiling at everyone she knew - and she knew most of the people in the synagogue. "Hi, Mr. and Mrs. Wise. Hi, Mr. and Mrs Ettinger. Hi, Mr. and Mrs. Levy." My father was beyond embarrassed. He was mortified, while I thought it was better than the greatest Purim parade in the history of our shul.

To bring it all full circle, when my oldest child Ethan was bar mitzvahed Ella was right there, sitting with the family, beaming with pride as if she were the surrogate grandmother who was somehow responsible for all the accomplishments of her grown up white children who surrounded her.

Every Chanukah she sent us a holiday card, and every year we responded with pictures of our children, who she loved watching grow up. After she retired from working for my mother she supplemented her income by making plaster of paris crafts and selling them in her neighborhood, and my mother sent her checks and helped her buy a car when her last junker gave out, and I'd send the occasional check, too, not out of guilt, but out of indebtedness.

I'm not sure what makes this a Jewish column. Perhaps it's our tradition of creating a legacy through memory, of keeping our loved ones alive in prayer and recollection. Perhaps it's because, over the years she taught me as much about family and commitment as anyone in my life. Perhaps it was because, through osmosis, part of her became Jewish, and part of me became, if not black and poor, at least softer, gentler, and conscious of what it means to love.

Healing The World One Self At A Time

This Rosh Hashanah I found myself going back to read and re-read a particular passage during the Musaf service. I wasn't sure why at the time, but this year, for me, the Days of Atonement have taken on new meaning.

"Love your neighbor as yourself; I am the Lord" (Leviticus 19:18). There is a Hassidic interpretation of the last words of this verse: "I am the Lord." – You think that I am far away from you, but in your love for your neighbor you will find Me; not in his love for you but in your love for him." He who loves brings God and the world together.

One meaning of this teaching is: You yourself must begin. Existence will remain meaningless for you if you do not penetrate it with active love and if you do not in this way discover its meaning for yourself. Everything is waiting to be hallowed by you; it is waiting to be disclosed and to be realized by you. For the sake of this your beginning, God created the world."

So many of my columns and, in fact, so much of our lives, turn outwards. Foreign affairs. National politics. Local agencies. Even writing about family is, in a sense, detachment from oneself. It's all viewing the world as an external process. When I write about Tikkun Olam – healing the world – it is usually in the context of charitable giving, or acts of kindness or a sense of justice. Again, these are all doing when the end result is action with or for the other. But what about us? What about me?

The great act of atonement we are all supposed to undertake this time of year is direct forgiveness, that is, asking all those we have wronged or may have wronged for their forgiveness. But isn't what we're really doing first is asking to forgive ourselves? Isn't the act of atonement, in many ways, an internal healing, an expiation through direct action, of the guilt of wrongdoing that causes us to stoop and stumble under its heavy load?

Years ago I was involved with an ashram in Ann Arbor, Michigan. I went to meditate and chant every day. The meditation was nice, but what really stuck with me was a simple concept: God resides in each of us. When we love God we are, in some way, loving that deepest, most mystical part of ourselves. We are validating the purest part of our being - our souls. And when we find God by loving our neighbor, we are loving ourselves by bringing peace of mind and peace of soul to ourselves.

You see, I can acknowledge this because I'm so good at keeping things focused on the external, and so bad at consciously loving myself. I sacrifice for my kids, say yes too often to volunteer work, and all my wife has to do is wink at me and I'm ready to drop everything and do whatever she asks. As for myself, well, I exercise – a lot. I read, usually late at night after everyone's asleep. I nap, occasionally, when I'm exhausted. But how often do I make like Ferdinand and take the time to smell the flowers? Not often enough.

As easy as it is for me to critique our local agencies, it's equally easy for me to listen to the critical voices in my brain that rapid fire negative, questioning remarks about everything I do and say. Don't say that. Don't do that. Why'd you do that? They're going to think you're a(n) (fill in the blank).

Active love. At this beginning point, the point in which we accept ourselves, love ourselves, we heal. As we heal we are able to love others and understand, rather than demean God by loving the world. It's in this moment of love and understanding that we can truly experience Tikkun Olam and heal the world. And in some miraculous way, as we move through the Days of Atonement into a new year, we create a new possibility for spiritual rebirth, for casting off the burdens of guilt and self hatred and coming to terms with God who resides in each of us.

Everything is waiting to be hallowed by us. For the sake of this our beginning, God created the world. May the New Year bless you all with a rejuvenated spirit of love and compassion. Shana Tova.

Sleeping With Strangers

There's a famous scene at the end of the film "Basic Instinct" in which Michael Douglas is in bed with Sharon Stone and nervous at the same time, because he might be sleeping with a murderer. Just as we begin to believe that she is, in fact, innocent, we see, under the bed, an icepick.

We are finding ourselves in similar icepick situations again and again, as a community, a people, even as a nation as Israel deals with the Palestinians. It's time that we realized, once and for all, that we have to be able to trust the people we lie down with, both before and after we "make love" to them.

My relatives from Tel Aviv were visiting us a few weeks ago, and their perspective on the Israeli political scene is one that is becoming more mainstream every day. They told us that they support Sharon even as they prefer the hard-line approach of Netanyahu, because, being pragmatists, they see that compromise and withdrawal from the settlements is the way of the future, perhaps the only way. They are happy, almost gleeful, that the pullout from Gaza is complete. Virtually no one with the exception of extremist settlers wanted to stay in that hellhole. The larger settlements on the West Bank will pose a greater challenge, but they believe that there will be change across the board. And as much as I hate to consider the possibility, there will probably be some give and take on Jerusalem as well, even if it only means annexing land and calling it East Jerusalem so the Palestinians can claim it as their capital.

"Understand, peace in Israel is not like peace in other countries," my cousin Danny told me. "Peace in Israel means no shooting civilians and no bombs. It doesn't mean partnerships or working together."

In which case, is it a sound peace at all? Or will it tumble down because its foundation is so weak, and the words of reassurance we need to hold onto are about as substantial as dandelion seeds, blown whichever way the wind happens to carry them?

Here at home the issue of peaceful coexistence and partnerships has also come to the fore. Orlando is home base for some of the largest evangelical organizations in the country. The Holy Land Theme Park isn't here by accident, or only because of the presence of Walt Disney World and Universal Studios. It's here because so many evangelicals call Orlando home.

The issue of how Jews and evangelicals relate is a perplexing one. On the one hand, we are and have been fertile territory for conversion, lest our souls, in the minds of the Christian right, be damned for eternity. On the other hand, the existence of Israel and the return of Jews from the Diaspora is a signal to many of the coming rapture, which is, after all, what many fundamentalist Christians look forward to. Without us, their salvation may not occur. On that basis, they love Israel and support her with cash and tourism. Sounds like we should be right there along with them, right? Unfortunately, it's not that simple.

Take Dr. John Hagee. He is the Founder and Executive Director of "A NIGHT TO HONOR ISRAEL" an event which expresses solidarity between Christians and Jews on behalf of Jerusalem, the State of Israel and the United States. This year the event will take place at the T.D. Waterhouse Arena in November. At the event Pastor John Hagee will present a $100,000 ambulance as a gift to the State of Israel. What's wrong with that? Nothing. Absolutely nothing. But what's wrong with getting in bed with fundamentalist Christians like Hagee? A lot more than you'd expect.

Hagee himself is an interesting character. He was awarded the "Humanitarian of the Year" award by the San Antonio B'Nai B'Rith Council, and the ZOA Israel Award by U.N. Ambassador Jean Kirkpatrick. Dr. Hagee has received numerous honors and accolades from national Jewish Organizations for his unwavering support of Israel. Quoting scripture on his website (**www.jhm.org**), he makes the Biblical case for support of Israel, as well as a hands off policy towards converting Jews. He says, "We believe in the promise of Genesis 12:3 regarding the Jewish people and the nation of Israel. We believe that this is an eternal covenant between God and the seed of Abraham to which God is faithful." He further states that Jews who follow the Torah are already saved. All other politics aside, Dr. Hagee appears, on the surface, to be the kind of devout Christian we could proudly call friend.

Unfortunately, this ignores his stand on many other issues, including but not limited to gay rights, civil rights, women's rights, abortion, prayer in the public schools, and many others. Are we willing to leap into partnership with someone who shares our love for Israel, but diverges with so many of us on so many other important issues? And of course we must acknowledge that the vast majority of fundamentalist Christians proselytize and attempt to convert as a foundation of their beliefs. Is it all right to support Hagee when he does believe in conversion efforts in the third world, just because he leaves us alone? I don't think so.

AIPAC may be able to show its support of anyone who gives to Israel, but it is a one issue lobbying organization. Zealous supporters of Israel may also be able to put their other beliefs on a back shelf, but I just can't. Orlando is the center of proselytizing and conversion efforts for numerous Christian organizations. We may say "thank you" for the donation of a life saving ambulance, but that doesn't mean we have to bend over and ignore the many ways we disagree, and the many reasons we can't actively partner. If I did I'd feel like I was making my bed with a partner who has a blade hidden beneath the sheets. That blade threatens so many aspects of my life and the values I consider central to my being I don't know how I could sleep with them. At best I'd lie down with my eyes wide open, uncommitted, on edge, prepared for any sudden movement that threatens my beliefs and my way of life.

2006

Ghost Ray

The Bat Mitzvah Series

I'm proud of my synagogue. While the process of becoming a bat mitzvah has not been an easy one, it has been entirely appropriate. My daughter's schedule, as is the case with so many children nowadays, veers from hectic to frantic. She practices her haftorah after school on the ride from home to the stable where she takes horseback riding lessons. She does her homework and studying after dinner until she goes to bed. So anything added to her already full plate feels like overload.

The bat mitzvah, and all the mandatory projects associated with it, tipped the scales. Would we have it any other way? For a short time anyway, absolutely not. She's baked challah. She's researched the meaning of her Hebrew name. She's read a book about Israel, and written a report on it. She's done community service at the Ronald McDonald House and groomed horses and mucked stables and led rides at Freedom Ride, a stable where handicapped individuals can ride horses. And of course she's gone to religious school and attended Shabbat services and bonded with the other kids in her b'nai mitzvah class at parties that are too numerous to name.

Now we're in the home stretch, the last thirty days before the big event. All the projects are done. She's learned her haftorah – a long one – and she's ready to start her torah portion. Our immediate families on both sides are coming in their entirety, something that didn't happen for my son's bar mitzvah. The only thing left for her to do is write a speech about her haftorah and the meaning of her bat mitzvah.

Which leads me to the most challenging, most meaningful part of this significant event.

Last week we met with our rabbi to discuss the main themes in this difficult, complex haftorah. It recounts the prophet Samuel's orders (from God) to Saul to wipe out the Amalekites. Not just their army, but their women, children, even the farm animals. Saul couldn't do it, and was punished for his decision to disobey God's commandment.

The tough part here is twofold. First, we like to think of God and loving and merciful, and second, it's hard to imagine slaying women, children, and animals.

Our rabbi helped us put this into a more modern perspective. He spoke to us about the need, no, the occasional mandate to wipe real evil off the planet. He spoke about not becoming evil in the process. He spoke about the different kinds of evil in the world, the kind we've successfully eradicated like polio and smallpox, the kind we're desperately trying to destroy, like cancer and diabetes. He spoke about mercy and compassion and what separates us from the lowlifes of the world.

And he asked about my brother. You see, my younger brother was just diagnosed with lung cancer. He has always been my best friend, my light bearer, my example of a good heart. Now he is my example of courage. He is planning to come to the bat mitzvah, and to ignore his presence, his plight, would be as inappropriate as turning a bat mitzvah celebration into a memorial service.

This is what our rabbi said. "Your brother is not gone. He is at the beginning of his treatments, and even though the road ahead may be rough, and there's reason to feel that life is unfair and sad, there's also reason to celebrate. Celebrate his life as well as your daughter's. Celebrate his being here. Celebrate family. Celebrate joy."

And that's what we're going to do. And that's why I'm proud of my synagogue.

To My Daughter
On The Eve Of Her Bat Mitzvah

Dear Jerica,

When I first thought of writing this letter to you, I paused and remembered doing the same thing for your brother when he was bar mitzvahed almost three years ago. I re-read that letter, and without going into what I said to him, I quickly realized that my message to you is totally different, though my love for you, my admiration and pride are equally strong.

Maybe it's because you're my only daughter, and as you've grown older and more beautiful I've come closer and closer as your overly protective father to wanting to lock you in a closet, away from the dangers of a male dominated world, until you're 35 or so. That being impossible, the next best thing is that you come into this world as a woman of strength and means, so that you're able to handle a world that too often still stinks of misogyny.

You have always had a smile on your face. May that never change. But the world gets tougher, and life gets harder as you get older. You're already finding that to be the case. What I want for you, more than anything, is that you never compromise your belief in yourself, you never accept second place because you're a girl, you never doubt your self worth, your integrity, your value. You've always been popular and well liked. Wherever you've gone, you've been surrounded by a group of girls who admire and appreciate you. It's no wonder. You're smart, fun, silly, happy, and easy to be with. It's an old cliché, but just remember that happiness does come from within, and your ability to hold your head up proudly – no matter what the rest of the world says – may determine your ultimate success.

I hope you never sell yourself short. If someone says a man's time is worth $100 an hour, but yours is only worth $61, don't buy it. It's not true. You are every bit as important and worthwhile as anyone else.

Why am I going into this issue of value and self worth so much? Because it seems to me that so many bright, extraordinary women diminish themselves and doubt themselves in the eyes of others, and it makes me sad to think you would ever do the same. Somehow I doubt you will. You've always believed in yourself, and my wish is for that to continue.

As far as your Jewish identity goes, amazingly, I'm not all that concerned. There's always the inkling of fear that you won't raise your children Jewish, but I have an innate belief that you will. From your tearful graduation from the Hebrew Day School when you said goodbye to your great group of girlfriends, to the easy commitment you made to your bat mitzvah studies, you have a central core of faith that is so different than mine was at your age. I was running from my Jewishness, and it took me years to come back. In fact, I was running from myself. All I wanted in high school was to fit in. I didn't want anyone to know how smart I was. I hid my test scores and talked, if not dumb, then simpler than I could. I didn't mention my last name. It was too Jewish.

You, on the other hand, have always had an internal joy and self confidence that I pray the world won't change. I don't see you running from anything, including your Jewish self, and that makes me so proud.

There are subjects, I know, that you will only talk about with your mother, and there are some that you won't even talk about with her. I'm grateful, even so, that we share so much, and when I'm shlepping you around from movies to horseback riding to Sunday School, I enjoy every moment. There are responsibilities that you will have in life that I will never fully comprehend. Motherhood, for one, which may be the most awesome experience of all. I'm sure, if you have children, that you will be a loving, patient parent, and that you'll ground your children in the values of tzedakah and tikkun olam – charity and healing the world.

So, my daughter, my beautiful light, on this day of you becoming an adult in the eyes of our Jewish community, I wish you the strength that comes from within. I wish you confidence and attitude. I wish that you always know with a certainty beyond doubt, how special and valuable you are, as both a woman and a Jew.

Searching For God In Small Places

I am in the midst of a faith crisis. Not an identity crisis, because I'm secure in my Judaism. Nor am I doubting my place at my shul, or the validity of anyone else's religious practices (though it may sound like that). I'm actively searching for meaning, and I'm struggling.

It may all stem from the death of my brother Ray, who was a profound believer in the survival of the soul in some form or other. And it may come, on the heels of his death, from my experience this year during the High Holy Days.

First, a disclaimer.

I am not disparaging anyone's beliefs in this column. I surely don't mean to negate or belittle in any way the meaning and significance other people get out of religious services. I am committed to my synagogue and synagogue life, and respect and appreciate my rabbi. I believe we all find meaning, simply enough, where we find it. And this year, for whatever reason, I've struggled to find meaning in services beyond my rabbi's sermons.

In the past, I looked around and felt connected to my Jewish kin as we confessed our sins during Yom Kippur, as we beat our chests in recognition of our shortcomings and guilt. Not this year. This year it fell flat for me.

In fact, I would rewrite Ashamnu. I wouldn't focus on the negative. I'd take a more positive approach. I'd say, "I'm good. I'm kind. I mean well and try to do my best, but sometimes I make mistakes. Sometimes I hurt someone. Sometimes I stumble and fall." That makes more sense to me than repeating a litany of offenses that have nothing to do with me. And if the answer is that we take on the collective sins of our community, perhaps it's time to take on the virtues as well.

The repetition, the constant praise of an all-powerful God fell on my deaf ears. I was bored and agitated, and as I looked around I don't think I was alone. For all the Jews who make a point of going to services twice a year, it looked like many were more anxious to leave than they were pleased to stay. Some of you may say shame on me. Some of you may feel I'm questioning the meaning you derived. Please don't. I'm not. I'm glad you found significance and felt renewed. I just didn't.

A cousin of mine said the High Holy Days services could be synopsized in three lines: God is great. God is everything. We are nothing. Sadly, that's how it felt to me this year.

I find myself oddly, quietly unsettled. I'm looking for meaning in the smallest things, the tiniest places, the softest sounds. I listen to grass crunch under my feet when I walk my dogs, to my six-year old practice a loud laugh, and I wonder about the balance of melancholy and joy. I look at a painting, drink a glass of wine, and am amazed, for a second, by the art of creation. I see the reflection of the sky in a lake and I ponder, briefly, what exists between earth and heaven. I am more impacted by my wife's smile than I am by saying Ashamnu one hundred times.

Let me tell you one experience I had recently that provided me with real meaning – meaning that touched my soul. You may say it's clichéd. You may call it a meaningless coincidence. I call it magic. My brother would have called it the power of the universe.

During Ray's funeral, at his gravesite, we all stood to say the Mourner's Kaddish. In the middle of the Kaddish a huge, colorful butterfly swooped under the tent over his grave. It nearly hit me in the face. It flew around his grave once, and even flew down around his casket. Then it took off and disappeared at the far end of the cemetery.

Not everyone at the funeral saw it, but those who did all had one thought. "Ray." I had the same flash. It wasn't cognitive, but rather just "flew" into my brain. Only afterwards did I pause and think, "Wow, that's weird, and isn't it silly of me to think that Ray was in that butterfly." But butterflies are symbols of transformation, and I'm convinced that a transformative process was occurring. For my brother's soul. For me.

I know you can't have experiences like that in synagogue on a weekly or even yearly basis. I know that many synagogues (mine included) are trying alternative services and new music to reach more people. I also know that real meaning comes when we find God in everyday life, in moments of hope and change. And hopefully, our faith can help us see the wonder and magic and awe of God, and give us meaning as we move through life and death. That's what I'm searching for, what I want to have faith in, where I want to find meaning, in the deepest, subtlest, smallest and most expansive places in my soul.

Memory And Beyond

I used to think that one of the great reasons to be Jewish was our focus on being here now, on doing good deeds on this earth in this lifetime for the sake of repairing and healing an imperfect world. Do good today, and leave the world a better place. That was enough. And it is still important to me, vitally important, but times have changed, and my perspective has changed, and suddenly, enough is no longer good enough.

Yitgadal v'yitgadal sh'mei rabah.

These words, the beginning of the Mourner's Kaddish, are some of the most often-recited, haunting, alliterative prayers in Jewish liturgy. I have always been told that Judaism doesn't emphasize an afterlife because we are judged by our deeds, not our words, and deeds must be done in this life, not the next. I was also taught that the way we live on is through the memories we leave behind. Through the recitation of prayers like the Mourner's Kaddish, through the collective memories and stories of family, we continue in our children and generations beyond. But something here has begun to trouble me.

B'almah dee v'rah cheer'utei v' yamleech malchutei, b'chahyeychohn, uv' yohmeychohn uv'chahyei d'chohl beyt yisrael.

Translated, the opening of the Kaddish means, "May his great name grow exalted and sanctified in the world that He created as He willed. May He give reign to his kingship in your lifetimes and in your days, and in the lifetimes of the entire family of Israel.

In the lifetimes…there's our connection to generations, through God and our commitment to what is holy.

And yet now, I think, there's something more.

What we recite is praise of God. What's missing is direct acknowledgement of those who have died, and what happens after. What happens to our souls?

I used to not concern myself with what came next. Maybe it's hitting 50. More likely it's been the experience of going through my brother's death, and believing, in a way that can only be described as faith, that he is paving the way for me to follow someday, and that he'll be waiting for me in some form or other, somewhere.

My brother Ray was a deep well, and thought long and often about death, which he called the next great adventure. He said it far better than I can, in an email he sent to a mutual friend more than six years ago.

"For me, life has taken a different turn. I continue to wrestle with survival issues, at work and in my personal life - the big picture, though, is not about survival. Survival issues seem to be the facade, the smoke and mirrors, the false myth that hides the truth. Truth is - and this is real truth - I'm ready to go at any time. I feel very complete these days. Feel like I've done what I came here to do. I guess there's still more to experience and create, cuz I'm still here. But, all the old unresolved dark clouds feel resolved, and my orientation these days feels clear. I'm not concerned about survival, I'm ready to be back in pure spirit form, ready for the next stage in the vast circle. Life continues, I believe, death of the body doesn't end the journey. I'm not limited to just this one body, this one time around, so no need to be concerned about survival.

The survival of the fittest thing is a myth. It's hogwash, because WE ALL SURVIVE. It's guaranteed. We never die, we just change form as we continue on our experiential journey. With that being the case - and I truly believe that this is the case - the only issue for me these days is, am I fully experiencing what is best for me to experience? For me, the real concern is not survival, it's choosing properly. And even that, when you get down to it, is OK. I'm learning to not judge myself so harshly (this is a tough one!) In the end, for me, the question continues to be, did I choose properly? Did I respect myself and others, did I treat myself and others properly? This is where love is the key. For me, love continues to unlock the correct door.

So that's me, today. Today, I'm a moonbeam! Play play play!"

My moonbeam brother, years before he got sick, found a key that ties us as Jews to the great beyond, the unknown after. By choosing properly, respecting others as we respect ourselves, we do right in the here and now. By living with love, we embrace the world. And by looking ahead without fear of survival we free ourselves from fear of today.

My cousin Roz told me recently that a Jewish scholar once wrote that the souls of all Jews today have been reborn from the souls of our ancestors who wandered in the desert. I like that because it acknowledges continuance, at least in some form. But I don't think we're limited to the souls of our wandering brethren. I think we're tied in to the universal souls of all those who lived righteously while they were here, and died lovingly, fearlessly, decisively when they moved on.

I am particularly lucky. Ray left me a legacy that is filled with memory and far more than memory. He left me a lifetime of his artwork - spiritual, joyful, transcendent works that revealed his soul on paper. He gave me an unexpected gift, and a new mission in life: to help him continue to live through his art. Watch out, world! Here he comes, and we'll all be better off for it, today, tomorrow, and beyond.

Y'hei shlamah rabah min sh'mayah,v'chayim aleynu v'al kohl yisrael, v'eemru: Amen. Oseh shalom bim'roh'mahv, hoo ya'aseh shalom, aleynu v'al kohl yisrael v'eemru: Amen

May there be abundant peace from Heaven, and life upon us and upon all Israel. Amen. He who makes peace in His heights, may He make peace, upon us and upon all Israel. Amen.

And that's the good word, today.

Today I'm a Jew. Tomorrow, a moonbeam.

Muslim Outrage Or Muslim Outage

A recent email made the rounds. I must have received it from four different sources. Whenever this happens I am immediately aware of something viral in the information being distributed. The people who saw it didn't want other people to miss an important message. Sometimes the message is a good joke. Sometimes it's photos of signs with stupid mistakes or funny billboards. And sometimes it's just something that your friends want to make sure you see. The "Muslim Outrage" email that flew around the world falls in the latter category. It hit home for me, too. Now admittedly, some of the noted incidents border on propaganda. When you're citing 125 shooting wars around the world involving Muslims as one of your points you're stretching things. But most of what was recounted, especially in light of the recent madness surrounding Danish cartoons, really struck a chord. If you happen to be one of the few who missed it, I'll fill you in on the major points made:

* Muslims fly commercial airliners into buildings in New York City. No Muslim outrage.

* Muslim officials block the exit where schoolgirls are trying to escape a burning building because their faces were exposed. No Muslim outrage.

* Muslims cut off the heads of three teenaged girls on their way to school in Indonesia. A Christian school. No Muslim outrage.

* Muslims murder teachers trying to teach Muslim children in Iraq. No Muslim outrage.

* Muslims murder over 80 tourists with car bombs outside cafes and hotels in Egypt. No Muslim outrage.

* A Muslim attacks a missionary children's school in India. Kills six. No Muslim outrage.

* Muslims slaughter hundreds of children and teachers in Beslan, Russia. Muslims shoot children in the back. No Muslim outrage.
* Muslims fire rocket-propelled grenades into schools full of children in Israel. No Muslim outrage.
* Muslims murder more than 50 commuters in attacks on London subways and busses. Over 700 are injured. No Muslim outrage.
* Muslims massacre dozens of innocents at a Passover Seder. No Muslim outrage.
* Muslims beat the charred bodies of Western civilians with their shoes, then hang them from a bridge. No Muslim outrage.
* Muslim newspapers publish anti-Semitic cartoons. No Muslim outrage.
* Newspapers in Denmark and Norway publish cartoons depicting Mohammed. Muslims are outraged.

All this death, all these murders and atrocities at the hands of Muslim extremists, Muslim terrorists, Muslim fundamentalists, and not a word of condemnation appears from an official Muslim source. After 9/11 the apologies from Muslim governments and religious sources were drowned out by the hordes dancing in the streets in Palestine and elsewhere in celebration of the symbolic downfall of Western society.

And now comes the coup de gras, what ought to go down in the annals of contemporary Muslim history as one of the most embarrassing moments of all time. Cartoons depicting Mohammad with a bomb in his turban set off riots the world over. The ironic complaint about the series of cartoons was that they portrayed the founder of Islam as violent. So what do Muslims do? They riot! They burn embassies! They torch cars and buildings! What message could be sent more ludicrously? It's sort of like complaining about exercising too much while running a marathon, or bemoaning the problem of overweight children in America while ordering from the drive through window at McDonalds.

I'm not saying all Muslims are extremist murderers, nor do I think the majority of Muslims feel no sadness or outrage when these horrific events occur. But when and how do they express it, even as the world watches a great religion make a spectacle of itself? I'm not sure which is worse, the most fringe elements of Islam taking over, or the good, decent middle of the road Muslims sitting back and saying nothing.

The email ended with a quote from Islamic writer Salman Rushdie, who wrote about these silent Muslims in a New York Times article three years ago. "As their ancient, deeply civilized culture of love, art and philosophical reflection is hijacked by paranoiacs, racists, liars, male supremacists, tyrants, fanatics and violence junkies, why are they not screaming?"

In this case, the lack of noise is deafening.

God Is Everything

I was taking my six-year old son Gabriel to school the other day when he started waxing philosophic. As his child's mind probes for understanding and order in his universe, he regularly opens doors we adults closed long ago. "Out of the mouths of babes" I thought. "Wisdom from unexpected sources."

Gabriel has a deep soul, and he and his Uncle Ray felt a kinship that was unique. We talked about his Uncle Ray's spirit, where it was now, and Gabriel said something like this: "Dad, I think that Uncle Ray has gone back to God. I think that when someone dies his soul goes back and becomes part of God again, and since God is in everything that means that Uncle Ray is in everything too. The sun. The trees. Even the buildings and rocks and streets all have Uncle Ray in them, because he's part of God. So I can talk to Uncle Ray wherever I am, because he's in everything, just like God."

I didn't have anything to say or add to that. What could I say, other than a sort of shallow "I feel Uncle Ray all around us, too." But Gabriel was saying something much more significant, much more profound.

I can remember all my Sunday school lessons about one God. I was taught that God is everywhere. God is all around us, I was told, one unified force, as opposed to the multiple gods of Hinduism or the father-son-holy ghost trinity of Christianity. The emphasis was on the where, not the what. What if God is everything? What does that do to us, and the way we deal with the world?

One thing it does is make a lot more sense out of the 613 mitzvot. Many of them, my rabbi once said in a sermon, are no longer relevant in our modern world, and many others are extremely mundane and particular. It's the number of commandments that strikes me. It's attitudinal. It makes the laws of kashrut make even more sense, because every bite of food takes on a special quality. It's looking at the world and seeing God in every act, in every object, feeling God in every breath, revering, not an all-powerful God of justice and consequence and destiny, but a God of life, of beauty, of creation. It's putting the holy in all aspects of our lives.

Imagine how differently we would live if, maybe not in every moment, but in every fifth or tenth moment we saw the holiness in the hand that smoothed the mortar between the building's bricks. Imagine if we looked through the window at the sunlight on oak leaves and bore witness to the magic of transparent glass and the wonder of light on leaf. Imagine if, driving down the road, we appreciated the holiness of the road, the car, the music, the cd, and our amazing ability to drive, listen, look, daydream and feel all at once. Imagine if we saw the holy in our enemies as well as our friends. Might that not change the Middle East all by itself?

Imagine if we reminded ourselves to occasionally look through a child's eyes and see God in everything. Every bite, every breath, every step taken and story told becomes something to hold as precious, something to care about and value. It's the Zen of Judaism. It's the manifestation of holiness in everyday life.

I have so many more questions than answers these days. I don't know about heaven or hell, rebirth or reincarnation or whether we simply drift off into a cosmic void. But I know I like the idea of the holy in everything. It changes the way I see. It's increasing my sense of gratitude. It's making the world a little more gentle and a lot more connected. And I can believe that, if God is in everything, the spirit never dies. It transforms.

And then yesterday Gabriel asked me, as I drove him to school, "Dad, what does God worry about?"

David Bornstein

2007

Old and New at the Western Wall

Why The World Needs Israel

Anyone who's Jewish and on any other Jew's mass email list has received emails like this: the most famous Jews you didn't know were Jewish, the number of Nobel Prize winners who are Jewish, the technological advances made by Israel, the exceptional health care in Israel, the map showing tiny Israel surrounded by huge hostile countries. And we've all heard that Israel is the only real ally of the United States in the Middle East, that, in fact, Israel is the only true democracy in the Middle East. These are some of the more obvious and common reasons to strongly support Israel.

But for the moment let's put aside the remarkable accomplishments of Jews throughout history, the amazing rebirth of the State of Israel in the 20th century, the incredible flowering of the desert as Israel truly became a land of milk and honey under the care of Jewish settlers. In a time when past president Jimmy Carter calls Israel an apartheid state, when Israel's enemies are arming themselves with nuclear capabilities that could wipe it off the earth, when the United Nations constantly (and shamelessly) decries Israel's treatment of Palestinians, let's consider why, on a higher level, the world needs Israel to exist, perhaps now more than ever.

For one, Israel's existence proves, day after day, that brains can win over brawn, that size doesn't matter, and that the skinny nerd, the little guy who always gets picked on, can stand up to the bully and succeed. Until the uprising of the Warsaw Ghetto, modern Jews were always viewed as the nebbish bookworms who would not stand up to defend themselves. We have a history rich with heroes, from David to Masada and the Maccabbees. But somewhere along history's road we lost sight of that heroism. Israel proved, from the War of Independence through the Six Day War to its struggle with terrorism, that a people with heart and hope and brains and morals can also be winners.

Today, of course, Israel has more of a reputation as a bully when it comes to its treatment of the Palestinians. But if that's the case, Israel is a unique bully, a compassionate bully. Israel is the only bully the world has ever seen that has given the lollipop back to the kid it beat up. Israel has set a remarkable example of compromise and courage by giving land to its enemies, to those it conquered. Did the United States or the Soviet Union do that after World War II? No, they divvied up the loot after emasculating the losers. What other country has ever won a war (multiple wars) and then exchanged land for peace? What other country has been big enough to not act like the victor? None that I can think of. All bullies should be so generous.

Israel is the only religiously based country in the world that protects, promotes, and accepts religious diversity. Sure, the United States protects the freedom of religion, but we are supposed to be a country that is not founded on the principles of any one religion. The Vatican doesn't accept any other faiths. And every country in the world based on Islam has become repressive and hostile to any other systems of belief.

Israel is the consummate example of benevolent acceptance. Muslims, Christians, Jews, the Ba'hai, all know that their important religious shrines are protected and open to them because of Israel. Yes, Israel is a Jewish state. Yes, you have to be Jewish to instantly be an Israeli citizen, and yes, if you are not Jewish you are still safe and able to practice your religion in Israel without fear or repression.

And finally, Israel is the only country in the Middle East that has ongoing debate about key policy issues that affect the future and fate of its citizens. No Arab country allows such strong and open dissent. Even the United States sees its politicians succumb to 30-second sound bites, to cautious and disingenuous responses to straightforward questions. Put two

Jews in a room and you get four opinions. It's an old, stereotypic line, but you know what? What's wrong with airing opinions in as frank and honest a manner as possible? Israel thrives on debate, and is the stronger for it.

What Israel can't become is the bully who remains a bully, who tears down houses without thought of reconstruction. Israel can't become a racist country, denying the rights of due process, justice, and equality to all citizens. And Israel must remain, as it has been, a light to the nations, a country with a conscience that grieves for all lives lost in a war, that heals anyone who comes hurt to a hospital, that treats all people as people, not as something less than.

When Israel's enemies clamor for her destruction, she must remain, more than ever, devoted to her ideals. It's then that this tiny country, this miniscule refuge of ethics and morality, sets an example for the world of what greatness really is, what the little guy can accomplish, what it means to be strong and compassionate, what acceptance and justice and integrity are all about.

The Way To Charity

A few months ago I was invited to visit an elementary school in Orlando. Richmond Heights Elementary is located in one of the more economically depressed areas of Orange County. It's an almost completely minority school, and is working hard to, as they say in these "no child left behind days," make the grade.

But it's a poor school, and their reality isn't ours. Richmond Heights is a Title I school. 98% of its students receive free/reduced lunch. In the homes where there are two parents, both of them work. Many homes are run by single parents. Many of these kids are latch key kids, coming home after school to a truly empty nest. There aren't the computers in the bedrooms and the books on the shelves we take for granted. All of this combines to create a home atmosphere that isn't conducive to learning, and the parents are too busy making a living, too tired after work to build a robust PTA. It's tough for a school to get the "A" rating it covets (which means more money, more support, more teachers) when it doesn't have parental support. That's the situation Richmond Heights faces.

Now add to that the fact that these children don't lead anything close to a privileged life. Many of them have never eaten at a sit down restaurant. They don't get to hang out at the Winter Park Shopping Village on Friday and Saturday nights. For them, a field trip is a visit to a supermarket, something they might never get to do were it not for school. A day trip to a petting zoo....forget it, too expensive. They can't afford the buses. They can't get parent chaperones (remember, almost all the parents work).

So then last week I got a call from their principal. She asked me if I could help raise the money to send the 4th grade class on a day trip to St. Augustine. They had not been able to make this trip for the past three years due to financial constraints. The total cost was $2,500. Could I help?

I sent out an email, a single email to a list of about 20 of my Jewish friends, and explained the situation. My wife and I started the fund raising with $250 of our own. Within 24 hours I had not only raised the money needed, I had exceeded it. People were glad to give. They felt good about contributing. They wanted to do the right thing.

What's that say about our own community's flat campaigns, our difficulty raising funds and getting people to ask for contributions? The answer is obvious, and speaks volumes to how we go about our fund raising efforts. The idea of giving to a communal pot and letting a committee decide where the dollars go isn't attractive. In fact, it's a distasteful deterrent, with no satisfaction for the donor. There's no goal met, nothing accomplished beyond meeting a campaign's numbers. Neither is continuing to supplement the general fund of non-profit agencies. Where does the money go? How is it used, besides subsidizing the bottom line, keeping staff employed, running the same old programs year after year? People want to give, and will gladly give, to programs they feel have a direct impact on those in need. When I sent a short email to people describing the immediate, positive results of a modest contribution (making a trip to St. Augustine possible for 10 year olds), they gave without hesitation.

This becomes a damning view of our community's allocations process. If we're looking for a better way to solicit dollars, if we want a feel good campaign, then we need to have specific programs that get direct support. People can then give to what feels right to them. As programs are funded, they are "closed" to contributions. The danger, of course, is that agencies wouldn't have money going to their general operating funds (but maybe that's not where our money should be going). Less "sexy" but still important programs might go unfunded. And agencies might skew their programming to those deemed more "sexy."

But these are issues that we can deal with. The bottom line is where the bottom dollar goes, and how we go about getting it. The path to greater charitable giving is right in front of us. Are we willing to take that first giant step forward?

Israel Lives

Every trip has its ups and downs, its highs and its disasters. Ours this summer had more disasters than most. I won't bore you with the details, but let's just say that leaving London we went to the wrong airport, spent $500 in desperation on a cab to the right one, had hotel issues, restaurant issues (neither of these in Israel), missed our flight on the way home, and then there was the Dead Sea. I'll tell you about that one.

We had a great guide for our first three days in Israel, a fantastic expert who I would recommend to anyone. His name was Dani, and he was bright and fun and kind and incredibly informative and interactive with our kids – the perfect fit. On our third day together we started early, visited Masada, hiked in the Ein Gedi Nature Preserve, swam in pools of water made by waterfalls and mountain streams, and then went down to the Dead Sea. Dani told us that there was brown mud near the shore that we could use to cover our bodies, but the really good black mud was out deeper, and that's what companies like Ahava use in their skin products. So we floated in the thick salty water, and then we went to immerse ourselves in mud.

The Dead Sea is an area of critical concern for Israel. Its water levels are dropping by three feet per year, because so much water that used to feed it is now being used for agriculture and for a thirsty, growing population. This is causing a number of problems, from even higher mineral concentrations in the already thick water to sinkholes, which are appearing around the edges of the Sea. As we waded out to the dark mud we sank almost to our waists in quicksand-like mud. We all got to a spot where we could use the gooey black mud to cover our bodies, but on the way back to shore we couldn't walk. We had to lie down and pull ourselves in, and most of the black mud washed off. I looked around and saw a pit near the shore. A brown pit. I thought that's what Dani was talking about, and I walked in. I didn't stop to think that no one was in it. There were no signs, and I traipsed in without thinking or hesitating. What I walked into was a thermal pit of scalding water and scorching earth. The skin on the bottom of my feet blistered off. I leapt back, but the sides of the pit were too hot to scramble back up, and in trying to grab hold of the edge the skin blistered off my hands. I started screaming for help. My kids didn't know what was going on. They thought I was joking. Finally, an Israeli saw me and pulled me out. "You fool!" he said. "What are you doing walking into a waste pit?!"

I limped back to the entrance. Dani and our driver took us the two hours back to Jerusalem, the closest emergency facilities, and I got a firsthand look at how our dollars are being used at the Hadassah hospital at Mt. Scopus. I was the only Jew in an emergency room full of Arabs who live in and around Jerusalem. The doctor who saw me (a young woman) was thorough, compassionate, and efficient. I was in and out of there in an hour and a half. With bandages on my feet and hands, wearing sandals, I looked like a Bedouin shepherd. Amazingly, the next day I was basically fine. My feet were blistered, but the Silverol cream (an Israeli product) they applied to me took away the pain and I healed quickly. We didn't miss a beat on our trip. I guess if you're going to be injured Israel is a great place to have it happen.

Now put this little story in perspective. Our trip could have been a disaster, but it wasn't. It's not just the incredible sites or the medical facilities in Israel that are outstanding. The fact is, there is enormous construction going on in Jerusalem and throughout the country – new roads, shops, office buildings. Understand that every night our older kids were out cruising Ben Yehuda Street, where hundreds, if not thousands of Israeli teens gathered. Envision the scene along the coastline of Tel Aviv, where families stroll and picnic and have cookouts virtually every night. Top it off with world-class restaurants that didn't exist when I visited as a child, and clubs and a music scene. And then walk streets that are both modern and connect you to the ancient history of our people. Israel isn't just alive. It thrives. Wherever you go, whatever you do, from the smoky cafes at night to the bustle of the Jewish Quarters in the Old City, from the emergency medical services to the great dining and hotels, Israel is exciting, dynamic, fun.

So now, when people talk about the blistering heat of the desert, it has new meaning for me. But disasters or not, we're looking forward to visiting the Galilee and the north next year. Nothing is going to keep us away for so long again. We must, I know, visit as often as we can to promote the vitality of this amazing land, and maybe even get a few of our tourist dollars to pay for new signage – in Hebrew and English - along the Dead Sea.

A Conversation With Sarah Palin

Recently this writer was lucky enough to have a frank, one-on-one discussion (in his mind) with Governor Sarah Palin, Republican candidate for Vice-President. Here's what she had to say:

DB: Governor Palin, there are those who question your ability to be an effective vice-president and mother of five. Can you comment, please?

PALIN: Well, David, in Alaska we have a saying, the best way to learn is with on-the-job training. That's why I know I'll be a good VP, because I'll learn as I go, and I'm a really quick study. Plus, that's why it's so great that my daughter is having a baby, 'cause she'll be right along side me helping out, one mom to another.

DB: I see. You've made it a point to speak favorably about women's rights and Title IX, the landmark legislation that barred gender bias in athletic programs at educational institutions across the country. Why are you, a woman who is opposed to a woman's right to choose, an advocate for women's rights?

PALIN: Well let me make one thing clear, David. I believe so strongly in women's rights that I believe we have the right to give up those rights, like our right to choose. I want the government to stay out of our lives in every way except when it comes to our own bodies. Then intervention may be necessary because, after all, we're just hockey moms who don't know better. And thank the Lord for Title IX. Without it I wouldn't be nearly so buff. I might even have that horrible under arm sag when I wave to all the people who love me.

DB: Rumor has it that you persuaded Senator McCain to open up the Arctic National Wildlife Refuge in Alaska for oil drilling. Is that true?

PALIN: I can't say I persuaded John. It was more of a wink-wink, if you know what I mean. Now when I hear all my supporters shouting "Drill Drill Drill" I just get so boiled up inside I can hardly control myself.

DB: Do you realize that this will potentially endanger a vast wildlife refuge, continue our dependence on oil, discourage alternative energies, and won't have an impact on our energy needs for a decade or more?

PALIN: Can you repeat the question?

DB: Let's talk about foreign policy for a moment.

PALIN: David, if I can interrupt you right there. I just want to say to all my critics who think I don't have foreign policy experience, not only can we see Russia from our Alaska shoreline on a clear day, as I've said, but it is often dark and shadowy over there, and if there's one thing we understand in Alaska with our long winter nights it's that daylight is better than darkness.

DB: Your point regarding foreign policy?

PALIN: Come on, you're joshing me. Isn't it obvious?

DB: Commentators have poked fun at your lack of understanding of the Bush Doctrine.

PALIN: Well let me correct that right now. John and I have had some very long discussions about the Bush Doctrine and I fully support it. I just needed to have it explained to me in plain old American English. John told me it's just God going out and spreading the rapture of democracy with two loaded barrels and a semi-automatic. So to all those nay-sayers out there, let me just say, "Now I get it."

DB: That's a very unique understanding. Finally, let's wrap this up with an issue that's near and dear to our readers hearts: your position on Israel and the Middle East.

PALIN: That's an easy one, David. At my church back home our pastor always told us, "If it was good enough for baby Jesus, it's good enough for us." That's why I'm such a strong supporter of the land of Israel.

DB: Thank you for that insightful perspective, Governor Palin. And that's The Good Word signing off until next week, when we explain the difference between Obama and Osama for those voters who still confuse the two.

2008

Stone Mandala

A Stone For My Brother

The Jewish New Year – Rosh Hashana – and Yom Kippur, serve as annual bookends for me, a period of time that has always been marked by reflection, contemplation, and hopefully, for those of us who take it seriously, an opportunity to ask sincere forgiveness of those we've hurt or wronged in some way. But since my younger brother was born and died around Rosh Hashana - a true New Year's boy – I look differently at these somber days, and my life and actions have also taken on a different shape.

Yahrzeits in September are filled with my last name. My grandfather Abe died on September 13, my brother on the 19th. My memories of my grandfather, who died when I was in fifth grade, are both scant and vivid. A blinding shock of white hair, thick pads of hands that sat heavily on my shoulders, soft wet lips that gave kisses I hated. The memories of my brother, on the other hand, take up my entire life.

We don't think very often about how our memories determine who we are as much as our present day actions, but they do. Almost all of what we do today, how we react, the decisions we make, are funneled through the lessons we recollect. We may be judged by others based on how we treat them on an ongoing basis, but we treat them based on how we have been treated by others over an accumulation of years.

I am one of the lucky few. I had a brother who was also my best friend, who always wanted to be with me, who followed me to college, who loved me and my family deeply, and yet resented the fact that the family I built took me away from him. Like you with your siblings, I have thousands of photos of me and Ray, posed, impromptu, playing together, staring at each other, on family trips as children, visiting each other as adults. And as much if not more than anything else in my life, his deep abiding love, friendship, and belief in me gave me the strength to believe in myself, the freedom to be who I am without fear that I would be forgotten, overlooked, ashamed or embarrassed.

The past two years since his passing have been an adjustment for me. There's a hole that will never be filled, no matter how much I'm loved by my wife and children. During the High Holy Days I look back now and remember, and recall what it was like to laugh and joke with him, to share on a level I'll never share with anyone else, and I rely on these internal pictures, these mental maps, to rekindle the spark of faith in myself that he created for me.

I think that's why a simple Jewish tradition has come to mean so much to me. Every year around the holidays, I go out to his grave, by myself or with my family, to look around and place a stone. Filled as they are with the bodies and markers of those we love, cemeteries are lonely places, and need the living to visit to make them less desolate and forlorn. The random plastic flowers, the anthills where the grass has thinned, the attempts to grow vines or other plants around tombstones only serve to accentuate how abandoned the dead often are.

So we leave stones to indicate that someone has been there, someone has visited and remembered. The tradition may reflect the biblical practice of marking graves with piles of stones, or even before that the ancient practice of placing large stones on graves so animals wouldn't desecrate the bodies. And stones became pebbles, and leaving something behind became a custom.

Last year my youngest son brought some fossils that Ray had bequeathed to him to mark the grave. This year we took stones from around our house. And every year we'll come back around the holidays, and I'll visit more often if I need to, to remind myself of who I was with him, who I am because of him, how grateful I am to have had him as my brother. Some holes never get filled, but we can still feel rays of light and love even as we stare up out of the dark. That is the beauty and miracle of memory, hallowed and acknowledged by one of our simplest and wisest traditions, as we leave a stone and say, "Here I am for you, who will never be forgotten."

When To Speak

I had the oddest experience this summer, something I hadn't dealt with in years. My son and I were in Raleigh, North Carolina for a baseball tournament (don't worry; this isn't about baseball). I was in the stands, watching the game and struck up a friendly conversation with one of the other dads. You have to understand; parents of athletes come from all walks of life, but in baseball and football the large percentage are members of the American working class – delivery men, truck drivers, plumbers and electricians and construction workers – the real muscle of America, if you will. So I was talking to this dad about our kids and where we were from and where we were staying. He told me he likes to stay at Holiday Inn Express, because you know what you're getting and he's discovered you can Jew them down and get a better price on a room.

Jew them down.

I knew what he meant. He was using "Jew" as another verb for "to haggle" or "to get something cheaper." I was dumbstruck. On the one hand, he seemed like a pretty nice guy. We were having a friendly conversation, and I didn't think he meant anything derogatory. He didn't know he was talking to someone who was Jewish. But it was derogatory. Jewing someone down epitomizes anti-semitic stereotypes. And I hadn't dealt with that kind of stereotyping in years.

I considered my dilemma. Do I confront him, let him know that I'm Jewish and don't appreciate my people and faith being categorized so offensively (imagine the world's reaction if we said we'd just Christed a bad investment , and it meant to sacrifice for no return, or we hoped our football team would Muslim the opposition, meaning to coldly murder them)? In return I could expect, what…a fight, a stupid argument, him walking away thinking I was a jerk? Or do I pretend he hadn't said anything wrong at all, let the conversation peter out, take a seat elsewhere and not deal with him again?

I chose the latter, the path of least resistance. The little voice in my head said it wasn't worth it. He was probably unaware he'd said or done something disparaging in the first place, and I didn't know him and would in all likelihood never see him again. And I've felt guilty ever since.

The fact that I gave up, not only on him, but on myself, has been gnawing away at me since that day. I know you can't pick a fight every time, fight every battle, battle every wrong and indignity. But there's a line, a very fine line that separates the consequences of action and inaction. It may be as small as heightening one person's awareness. Or it may be as large as intervening sooner in a world war and saving millions of lives.

The issue of standing up and taking action permeates our definition of self. When we choose to act, we define who we are and what we believe. I've thought about this every time I choose to write or not write a letter to a congressman, or when I vote. I've considered it when I decide to make a contribution or forego making one to a charity. I've asked myself what my values are when I do something (or nothing) about global warming or poverty or disease. I've asked myself how much I love someone when I choose to sit back instead of confronting them to live every day to its fullest.

The ramifications are endless. But the choice, I believe, is straightforward. In almost every situation, it's better to act than not. Better for your soul. Better for your family and friends and companions. And ultimately, better for the world. It's all right not to do it all. But it's never all right to always sit passively by, to never connect, never commit, never confront. The Jewish way defines being here now, in the moment, taking responsibility for our actions, and understanding the consequences and failures of sitting on our hands.

I missed an opportunity to change the world one person at a time. I won't give up on myself and miss that chance again.

Real Community

It isn't often I'm so moved by a religious ceremony that I feel compelled to write. But at a special bat mitzvah a few weeks ago at Congregation Ohev Shalom I was more than moved. I felt transformed. The situation was unique, as is the child involved.

We attended a Monday morning service for Talia Finer, daughter of Paul and Teresa Finer. Puns aside, there isn't a finer family in Central Florida. Paul is an anesthesiologist, and has been our go to guy when we need a doctor's referral or help in ER. Teresa is an attorney specializing in immigration issues. Both have been friends of ours for years, and involved in all aspects of Jewish communal life, from volunteer work at the Federation to involvement with the Hebrew Day School and other agencies. They are generous with their time and philanthropy, and Teresa was kind enough to forgive me when I recommended a car (the make of which shall go unnamed) she subsequently bought and hated.

They have three daughters – Elena, Talia, and Anna. Talia, the bat mitzvah, was born with special needs. She's an intense, bright girl, and without going into detail has long term issues - a complicated combination of developmental issues from birth - that the family has dealt with compassionately and head on. So having her become a bat mitzvah presented its own challenges. Talia and the synagogue both rose to the occasion. Talia led the service, read three Torah portions, gave a speech, and blatantly, obviously soaked up the love and joy that surrounded her.

What was so special, so unique about that Monday morning service? Let's forget the fact that the sanctuary was packed. Let's forget the number of times people (myself included) cried during the ceremony. Let's forget the spontaneous and lengthy applause that erupted from the congregation as Talia fulfilled her duties as a bat mitzvah. What was so special about that morning (one that I will never forget), was the sense, as I looked around, of community, that we were all sharing a moment in time, that we were active participants in the spiritual growth and happiness and awareness of a young, amazing girl. From the support Talia received from Cantor Robuck, the education director Amy Geboff, and her tutor Ellen Zollman, to the outpouring of attention and love she received, we were all in this together, a congregation bent on one thing and one thing only: wanting Talia to succeed.

What was so amazing about Talia's performance? For the record, Talia loves services, and if you sit near her you can't help but notice as she participates loudly and boisterously. Torah portions aside, that morning she did certain things I have never seen before on the bimah. As she sang responsive prayers she looked up at the congregation, taking it all in, and then looked back down at her prayer book to recite her part. When she was standing at the bimah waiting to chant her prayers, she sometimes stood with her forehead leaning against her left hand. I don't know whether she was overwhelmed by the experience, trying to contain herself, or just resting, but it was touching and poignant to watch her, head in hand, working so hard to take her place within the Jewish world.

And then there was Rabbi Rubinger's sermon. Rabbi Rubinger began by announcing that he'd been asked by Teresa, two days prior to the service, if he would give a sermon. He agreed to do so, obviously a bit grudgingly (it's a lot of work) and with some reservations. But, he said, what he had written failed to capture the preciousness of the moment. So he spoke off the cuff with brilliance and love about three elements that were bound together that morning: the power of community, the power of the individual, and the power of love.

During the brunch that followed I wandered around with my wife, wondering what to do with the rest of my week. Where could I go from here but back to reality, back to normalcy after being so uplifted on a Monday morning?

Reality and normalcy did return, of course, and far too quickly, but not without realizing that a part of me had been permanently changed by my synagogue, my rabbi, my friends and fellow congregants and one special little girl.

When The Parent Is The Problem

Many years ago I attended my first regional United Jewish Appeal meeting in Atlanta. I was, at the time, on the leadership track for our Orlando Federation, and officers on the board time thought it would be a good experience for me. Much of that weekend has been folded into the dim recesses of memory, but one moment stands out. Near the end of the weekend a broad discussion took place about "that year's emergency campaign." Every Federation was going to be asked to raise money to rescue Ethiopian Jews, and the costs were staggering. I remember sitting there thinking, "Another emergency campaign to justify the parent company's existence. What will the emergency be next year?"

I don't think we ever participated on any scale in this campaign. And I don't want to in any way diminish the need to help and at times rescue Jews abroad. There is a need, and Federated communities have performed miracles of aid and assistance. But there is a broader, deeper question that must be asked firmly and answered squarely. Is the parent organization to our Federation – United Jewish Communities - still relevant, or has it outlived its time?

At its inception about a century ago the United Jewish Appeal had a huge reason to exist. Jews were moving to Israel. World War II erupted. Israel was created. There was war with neighboring Arab countries. It became, in time, the second largest philanthropic organization in the United States (next to United Way). There was much to do. Jewish populations were decimated. Jews in the Soviet Union and other countries were being persecuted and needed help. Israel needed trees, needed water, needed support in every aspect of life, from political and military support to fundamental social services. And so the annual campaign had a meaning and a message and a purpose, and it grew, and people felt good about giving. In fact, giving felt vital, a part of the core value system of Jewish communal life.

United Jewish Communities was formed in 1999 from the merger of United Jewish Appeal (UJA), Council of Jewish Federations (CJF), and United Israel Appeal (UIA). While there have never been any thoughts of malicious or dishonest acts, since that time the organization has had an unfortunate reputation for being inefficient and ineffective. In an article posted in The Forward magazine, Anthony Weiss wrote that "UJC's current president and CEO, Howard Rieger, has attempted, since taking office in 2005, to restructure and streamline the agency, but his tenure has been marked by turmoil. A number of senior professionals have left UJC since Rieger's arrival; the local Detroit federation is in rebellion over its dues to UJC, and several other federations have protested the dues formula. Meanwhile, the annual fundraising campaign has stagnated, and allocations to overseas beneficiaries, the charities' signature cause, have been dropping. The organization has also been accused of being closed and resistant to criticism."

In a blog called "Disunited Jewish Communities," an inside UJC source says that "Those of us inside the organization didn't need a Survey to know that morale has never been lower, that more resumes are in circulation 'on the street' than ever before, and that UJC's top professional leadership wants no data that would conflict with their perception that everyone at UJC is happy, happy, happy," wrote the contributor, identified as "UJC Boys/Girls." Closer to home, there are significant issues that we must face vis a vis our relationship with our parent umbrella organization. Membership dues to UJC are calculated on the basis of population size and size of campaign. Communities with either a disproportionately large Jewish population and a small campaign (Orlando) or a large campaign and a shrinking population (Detroit) are hurt by the formula. Our local dues are about \$80,000/year. This number has been buried in our overseas allocation, and means that we don't give as much overseas as we think, and quite honestly, we have never gotten \$80,000 worth of services from UJC. And while UJC still funds a variety of important programs globally, I have to ask: could we do a better job allocating these dollars ourselves? If we cut our dues to UJC by 50% or even 75%, and took that money to hire someone whose sole purpose was research of overseas programs for us to directly fund, would our dollars be better spent and have greater, more positive impact? I think the answer is yes.

There comes a point in time when an organization struggles to find reason to exist, and then justifications and rationalizations ensue. There's a reason the annual campaigns are flat and struggling across the nation. They are attempting to strike a chord with current donors based on past appeals that no longer resonate with relevance. There is still a need for tikkun olam – for healing this world and helping Jews in many countries and in all aspects of life. UJC just hasn't figured out a new way to do it. It's time we look at our relationship with our parent company, and ask ourselves if, having grown up in a new age, we can't do a better job on our own.

2009

Meditating Woman

Coke Or Pepsi

I attended the bar mitzvah of the son of some good friends of ours this past week. It was, by all accounts and impressions, a wonderful, satisfying weekend. Charming, teary, endearing – it had all the characteristics one hopes for in a meaningful Jewish event.

The focus of the party Saturday night was on teens – the bar mitzvah boy and his friends, who were, as is the case for thirteen year olds, awkward, precocious, beautiful in all the ways that make parents both proud and scared to death. Maybe it was my mood that night, for I felt a bit distracted, unfocused. Maybe it was because we're all going through such hard times right now that I brought some of that heaviness into the party with me. I found myself fixated on, not the sweet candle lighting ceremony or the tight bonds the bar mitzvah family has with their closest friends, but on Coke or Pepsi.

That's right. The game played by kids at every bar or bat mitzvah party I have attended in the past ten years. I don't know who invented it, though I imagine whichever party planner you ask would take credit for it. Ohmygod, I remember thinking, here we go again while I, an adult at a kid party, eat my dinner and watch Coke or Pepsi. Kids in two lines on opposite ends of the dance floor racing across to sit in laps, bow down to the bar mitzvah boy, lock arms, hop on one leg, all at the crazy verbal cues of the MC. "Coke!" he yells. "Pepsi!"

And every kid participates. And every one, wanting to appear mature but being in fact only thirteen, having a great time. And watching in the shadows, I asked myself how thirteen year olds always stay the same, while I've grown old(er), cranky(er), more set in my ways.

And then I was hit again, this time by an epiphany that shook me out of my doldrums. It's not about things staying the same, or me getting older, or the games kids love to play. It's about choice. The teens at these parties make a conscious choice to participate, as difficult as it may be for the shyest among them, as clumsy and tongue-tied as the boys may be, as flirtatious and frightened as the girls may be. The bar mitzvah boy, somewhere along the way, made a decision, a conscious choice (with prodding and assistance, no doubt, from his parents), to do the necessary work and spend the lost afternoons studying his haftorah so that he could become a man (albeit a very young one) in the eyes of the Jewish community. And we, as Jews, have been taught since we were little, that it is the choices we make in our lives that matter. Not hope for an afterlife. Not a casual forgiveness of sins committed, hurts caused, but our actions borne out of the decisions we make every day that make a difference.

These days, those decisions come with a price tag attached, and often a painful one at that. I know I'm not alone in making choices that affect me, my family, my community. The economic downturn has forced us all to ask difficult, heart wrenching questions. And we may not want to hear the answers. Have we sacrificed enough, cut back enough? Do we have to sell our house, move to another city, in order to meet a shrinking household budget, in order to find a new job? How much can we give to charity this year, for it surely won't be what it has been in the past? How can we be happy and make do on so much less? The answers that Judaism teaches us are simple and hope-filled. We have. We do. We are. We can. We will.

All of us, in these hard times, have hard choices to make, choices that effect lives. And all I can say is thank God we all have a community that stands behind us to bolster us, agencies to assist us, friends to support us, faith to heal us and remind us that we are strong, that once we made the walls of Jericho tumble, that we can persevere by acting rightly, appropriately, with humility and dignity today. And if we can remember the miracles that saved us, the strength that resides in each of us, the acts that define us, then we can survive, whether it's through an economic collapse or an uncertain future. That's why traditions matter, why some things should always be. Coke or Pepsi. It's not about winning the game, but about choosing to play. We need to remember that it's the choices we make that make a difference and determine who we are.

A Radical Idea For Muslim Radicals

For weeks now, ever since Israel began its military offensive against Hamas, the world has risen up and denounced the action, focusing on the destruction of Gaza's infrastructure and the spilled blood of innocents, conveniently forgetting years of missile attacks and homicide bombers who targeted civilians. All this while Israel has actually warned residents of Gaza about the imminent bombing of buildings to protect uninvolved residents' lives.

Israel will, in all likelihood, agree to a temporary truce. And foreign funds will pour into Gaza. And rebuilding will begin. And Hamas will also rebuild, and rise up, and start lobbing missiles into southern Israeli towns, and strap bombs onto young men and women and blow them up in Israeli schools and markets and nightclubs and cafeterias. And Israel will retaliate once more. And the cycle of death and despair will be renewed. And so it goes.

Amidst the bloodshed and bombing and battles an anniversary took place, one largely unnoticed, but nonetheless incredibly significant in world history. It was sixty years ago that Martin Luther King, Jr. visited India, and had his faith affirmed and his vision clarified. The path he would blaze in leading African Americans into an era of equality was both historic and permanent. There was no going back. He saw the results of the life and teachings of his personal hero and "guru," Mahatma Gandhi, and he saw that it was good, and made sense, and could be imported back to the United States with great effectiveness. That was the use of non-violent tactics to affect widespread social change.

We take it for granted. Rosa Parks sat on a bus and refused to give up her seat. Protesters sat in front of stores and marched peacefully down Main Streets across the South. Millions gathered and listened to a dream. The Civil Rights Movement moved from private parlors to public pronouncements, from a curiosity to a commitment, and today we have a President born of a white mother and black father who will lead our nation in a time of tremendous need.

I never thought I would use this column to make a recommendation to Hamas or Hezbollah or any terrorist organization, but as I read about King's trip to India at the same time I saw images of blasted buildings in Gaza, a light bulb went off. If Hamas truly wanted world opinion to shift in its favor, to be seen as a representative of Palestinian rights and autonomy, an alternative path exists for it to take, one that disavows the use of human bombs and bloodshed, one that Israel (and the world) would have to respect and recognize. That is the path of peace.

Not reconciliation. Not overt compromise. Not caving in to all of Israel's demands. But rather, by turning its cheek, by laying down arms and taking up the banner of pacifist resistance, these terrorists who are in fact the world's greatest cowards, who willingly sacrifice children, young men and women while they spew hatred and hide in tunnels and caves, would transform their cause into one of righteous nobility.

This doesn't mean I believe that they would get everything they want. It doesn't mean I want terrorists to take over. But it does mean that there might be another way for Palestinians to get some of what they want: independence, sovereignty, stability, prosperity, peace.

Imagine for a moment if residents of Gaza chose to no longer work as minimum wage laborers in Israel. Imagine if they peacefully stood by the protective wall erected by Israel or the roads that were built so that Israelis could have safe passage around the county. Imagine if all their violence ceased, and they simply sat down in front of Israeli soldiers. I believe that Israel would take notice. I believe that our people are so grounded morally that we would say, "Bravo, now it's time to talk." I believe that real change, in whatever form it finally took, would occur.

It's a radical thought, for radicals who have espoused the absolute and total destruction of Israel from day one, to suddenly become advocates for peaceful resistance. And truthfully, I don't think it will ever happen. But wouldn't it be amazing if it did? And wouldn't Martin Luther King Jr. and Mahatma Gandhi's souls stir and take notice? And so, I think, would Israel, and so would we.

Open Your Heart

Besides the spiritual renewal, the chance to begin again and the hope for a new year filled with promise, one of the "perks" of the High Holy Days, for me, are the special sermons we all hear. I know. Am I crazy? Don't I fall asleep? Aren't they interminably long? Maybe I am nuts, but I listen, and generally, I learn something, and benefit from listening.

This year, on Kol Nidre, I heard a sermon about communication – with one another, and with God. Our rabbi spoke about all the ways we in modern society miss one another – the emails, the text messages, the tweets, the messages on answering machines instead of the humanity of direct, personal connections – a conversation, a phone call, listening to and sharing with one another. How many of us, he asked, are grateful when we can leave a message instead of making small talk? How many of us use email to avoid having a difficult conversation? Too many of us, it seemed, by a show of hands. He quoted from Bruce Springsteen, and it was apropos:
"You might need somethin' to hold on to
When all the answers they don't amount to much
Somebody that you can just talk to
And a little of that human touch. . ."

It all rang true for me. But I kept waiting for the last major point to be made, and either I missed it, or the sermon did – how do we communicate with, how do we connect with God?

Now I have to admit something. I'm not sure that I believe in God, at least not the traditional almighty God, the being who is everywhere and knows all, watching over us, judging us with supreme benevolence. I do believe in the forces of nature, in the abundance of life. I believe we're not alone, and I believe that there are laws of order and physics that shape existence. I believe in the transcendence of goodness, in the presence of evil, in being open to what the universe has in store. But is that God? And if it is (or if it is one possible definition) how do we touch it? Where is the connection that transcends our physical limitations and takes us....somewhere else? Somewhere we become more than we normally are?

Our rabbi also quoted Marshall McLuhan, the famous profess of communications. In McLuhan's seminal work, "Understanding Media – the Extensions of Man," he proposed that the media itself should be studied, not only the content they carry. This has been popularly quoted as "the media is the message." If that's the case, then when we reach out to God, we are both the message bearer and the message. And if that's the case, is the message so important, or the fact that we, as human beings, choose to seek it out, discover and ultimately deliver that message to others?

This is particularly relevant for me after the long (and in my mind, repetitious) services of Rosh Hashana and Yom Kippur. I'm sure all of our local rabbis have good reasons for the structure and repetition of our religious services, but if the important thing is not the prayer, but that we choose to pray, if the point is our presence at shul, not our performance, then perhaps, by being the vehicle for prayer, we are putting ourselves in position to experience God.

I know for myself that the experience is the message. I know that when I am at my most empathic and vulnerable (which some might say isn't very), when I allow myself to feel what's going on around me without barriers or borders, I come closest to communicating in a godly way. When I have experienced the most special moments of my life, looking out over a mountain range after a long day's hike, seeing the many ways my wife expresses her love for our children, stopping to breathe, to listen, to be aware of my place in a moment, when I open my heart and let the world in - that's when I think I come closest to touching God. And if we do that just a few times this year, if we make the choice to become the media for the message, if we make the effort to step out of the ordinary in our daily lives and open our hearts, we may find a way to communicate with our personal God, and in the process, touch a deeper, more profound, truer part of ourselves.

Who Is A Jew?

Two separate and distinct incidents occurred recently that compelled me to ask the question, "Who is a Jew?" I feel nervous just writing the words, as I step into territory best left to rabbis and theologians, those far wiser and more versed than I in this basic, complex issue that strikes at the core of contemporary Jewish life. I am no expert or authority, nor do I pretend to be. I am merely inquisitive, perhaps dangerously so, and so I ask, so we can explore together.

The first event took place at a book review chaired by my mother, Rita Bornstein. The guest lecturer that night was Greg Dawson, once a columnist for the Orlando Sentinel who has published a book titled, "Hiding in the Spotlight: A Musical Prodigy's Story of Survival, 1941-1946." The book is about Dawson's then-Jewish mother, who with her sister survived the Holocaust by both pretending to be Christian and performing, playing piano for Nazi troops. Dawson was raised non-religiously, though his family celebrated Christmas and Easter. He didn't know his mother had been born Jewish until much later in his life, and when he found out that he could be considered a Jew he called it "an upgrade," because he now had a distinct, and special identity. But when I asked him if he ever considered the fact that, in another time and place, he and his daughters would have been rounded up and executed as Jews, and if that affected his world view, his face went blank, and he replied, simply, "No, the thought never occurred to me." In other words, in his lack of introspection, he missed the point entirely.

And then, more recently, a disturbing legal case in Britain was brought to my attention. In a decision with far reaching implications, a court in London concluded that basing admissions to a private Orthodox high school on a classic test of Judaism — whether one's mother is Jewish — was by definition discriminatory. Whether the rationale was "benign or malignant, theological or supremacist," the court wrote, "makes it no less and no more unlawful." The court ruled that it was an ethnic test because it concerned the status of the applicant's mother rather than whether the 12 year old boy, whose father was Jewish but whose mother converted to Judaism, considered himself Jewish and practiced Judaism.

Who is a Jew? My wife is a Jewish convert, and is a committed, practicing Jew. And my two oldest children were converted, in a ceremony held in the waters of the Wekiva River. Is my wife Jewish? Are my children, who went to the Hebrew Day School and were bar and bat mitzvahed, Jewish? I dare anyone to say they are not. And yet in their cases, while the British courts would probably conclude that they are Jewish, Orthodox Jews would say they are not, because their mother, my wife, converted in a Conservative synagogue. I also have a niece and nephew, who do not incorporate anything Jewish into their daily lives, but whose mother was Jewish. Are they Jews? Again I would say yes they are, not because of who their mother is, but because, when asked, they would say that they are.

This leads me to my first conclusion, which in some ways coincides with the British courts. I don't believe it is how you are born that makes you Jewish, but how you live. I know this goes against a great deal of Jewish history and scholarly thinking, but Judaism has survived for thousands of years because it has been able to both embrace important traditions and change with the times. And now, as we concern ourselves with intermarriage and connection and the future of Jewish identity, it is time we reevaluate what makes us who we are.

I believe we are the chosen people, not because God chose us, but because we choose to be Jews. We place ourselves in the line of fire. We risk being singled out, and we do so bravely and willingly. We make a conscious choice that excludes us, differentiates us, distinguishes us in the eyes of the world. Are we different, smarter, richer, better? No. We are, like any other group of people, richly varied, distinguished in our differences, exclusive in our self-awareness, our identification as a minority, and our core ethical and spiritual values.

When Rabbi Hillel was asked to teach a man all of Judaism while the man stood on one foot, Hillel replied, "Do not unto others as you would have others do not unto you. The rest is commentary."

This core value, that dictates how we live and treat one another, may be the heart of being Jewish. But I would go further. Our willingness to say we are Jews, and in so doing taking on a mantle of responsibility and a burden of hatred by so many others, makes us who we are. Are Jews for Jesus Jewish? No, they are Christians in sheep's clothing, claiming to be Jews but living Christian lives and accepting Christian beliefs. Is Greg Dawson Jewish? No, because he doesn't look in the mirror and identify himself as a Jew. And my wife and children are Jewish to their very bones, because in their souls they know they are. Because they live Jewish lives. Because they choose, without a doubt in their hearts, to be Jews.

Hat Trick

Three years ago I took a group of my best friends and closest family on a fly fishing trip to Montana to celebrate my 50th birthday. There were only two conditions: all guys, and my guests had to pay their way there and back. I handled all the rest of the expenses. We were a fun, eclectic group. A close friend from high school. A nephew. A cousin. My oldest son and my brother. My best friend from college. My brother-in-law. My best friend since college. One of my closest friends since moving back to Orlando, and my best friend from my Disney days. We fished for two days on the Little Bighorn, and caught and released hundreds of trout. We boated for a day on a reservoir that looked like a mini-Grand Canyon. We played poker at night, and drank good wine and ate great food and laughed and told stories and caught up on our lives. It was the last adventure of my brother's life. A perfect time.

It wasn't long before I started taking notes. It seemed everyone had something brilliant to say, something hysterical, something off the cuff. I began to collect lines, and planned to turn them into a memento poster at the end of the trip. "How do you feel about handguns?" "When I was 8 I stole a box of raisins." "See, I can walk a straight line." "That's the look of a man who wishes he'd had a vasectomy earlier." "I don't follow norms. I live outside the lines." "I just paid the bill. Who wants to give me mouth to mouth?" And the line that got repeated the most by all: "Give him the f---ing hat!"

You see, a few people brought presents, though it wasn't requested. Books, a Mexican sombrero, a fishing vest. But what I fell in love with out there under the sun as we floated down the river was my cousin Sam's hat. He wore the coolest looking water buffalo hat that he'd picked up on a trip to South Africa. It was a Crocodile Dundee sort of hat, with a natural swagger to its curved rim, a soft and mottled texture unlike any hat I had ever seen. It looked good on everyone who wore it, and I told him how much I liked it. My friend David overheard me, and since Sam had not given me anything as a birthday gift David got a great idea. "Give him the hat." He went further. "Give him the f---ing hat. You're gonna give him the f---ing hat." For two relentless days David pounded Sam. And Sam didn't, couldn't give up the hat. He was too attached to it. No hard feelings. I understood. It would have been an extraordinary gesture.

The trip ended. Our lives returned to normal. My brother passed away. But the story of the hat remained.

Then, just a few days ago, unsolicited and out of the blue, a box arrived at my door, and in the box was the hat, with a note from Sam. "I've been meaning to send this to you for a long time," he said. "Here's hoping that this brings you good times and new beginnings." I was stunned, overjoyed in the simplest way. It brought back memories of the time we spent at the lodge, on the river. It made me think of all the people who are most important to me. And I think, I hope, maybe, that Sam is right.

This is a time for new beginnings, a time to put aside old ways, to put on something new, to take on a different look, a different approach, and begin again. The recession has many of us down, hanging our heads, worried about tomorrow, about survival. I'm one of them.

But I also am one who believes in change. I believe, as day follows night, that life will get better. I believe we can shift our destiny, crawl out of old habits and old ways and use this difficult, sometimes devastating time as an opportunity. I'm looking at this new world in a new way. I'm stepping back, and as I've often pushed our community, I'm pushing myself to make a paradigm shift and move forward, outside the lines. I'm doing something I've always dreamed of – I'm starting to write a book, for fun, with my youngest child as inspiration. I'm beginning. I'm starting from scratch. And I'm scared and hopeful that life and our world will turn around.

So this is it, for me, the conclusion to this season of writing. I accomplished some of the things I wanted, and others remain on the bookshelf, waiting to be dusted off for a future column. I believe times have changed. I'm wearing my f---ing hat with a little swagger in my step, and keeping my eyes open for the next great adventure. I wish you well. Have a great summer, and if you can, make it a great beginning.

2010

Live Mailbox

David Bornstein

If There Were No Israel

On the eve of his visit to the Middle East, United States special envoy George Mitchell threatened that the US would freeze its aid to Israel if the Jewish state failed to advance peace talks with the Palestinians. Prime Minister Netanyahu responded by saying that, if the United States did not provide the loan guarantees to Israel that it had it the past, Israel would move on. Israel would survive.

At the same time a rank undercurrent has swelled among certain political and intellectual groups who espouse the position that, were it not for Israel, Islamic terrorists would have no target for their rage, and peace would reign in the Middle East.

So let's take a brief look at that scenario. We're not assuming Israel's destruction, for that would have far reaching social, moral, and political implications. What would the world look like if Israel simply vanished?

First of all, the world would be missing the greatest technological/entrepreneurial engine that currently exists. Netanyahu's economic reforms and a million Russian immigrants have shifted many Israelis away from public life and into commerce and technology. Tel Aviv has become one of the world's entrepreneurial hotspots. Israel has more high-tech start-ups per capita than any other nation on earth. It ranks second behind the U.S. in the number of companies listed on the NASDAQ. Israel attracts as much venture capital as France and Germany combined. Between 1980 and 2000, Egyptians registered 77 patents in the U.S. Saudis registered 171. Israelis registered 7,652.

How would Gaza fare? Well, in 2009 Israel delivered more than 630,000 tons of humanitarian aid to Gaza. That would disappear. So would the 24.5 million gallons of diesel fuel Israel gave to Gaza last year. The 10,000+ Gaza residents who went to Israel for medical attention would have to look elsewhere. So would the 20,000 Gaza residents who entered Israel for work.

Oh, and by the way, the only democracy in the region will have vanished. And since fundamentalist Muslims would still hate the trappings of Western civilization, these Arab leaders would have to find someone else to hate, some other country to scapegoat. Can you say USA?

Palestine would still be underdeveloped as are nearly all the Arab states, whose combined gross domestic product is less than that of Spain.

Nearly 50% of all Palestinians would still be unemployed. The animosity between the 85 percent of Muslims who are Sunnis and the 15 percent who are Shiites would not cease or vanish.

Egypt would still persecute its Coptic Christian minority. Iraq would still covet Kuwait. Iraq and Iran would still hate each other and every so often go to war. Iran would still be run by the ayatollahs.

Al-Qaida, largely funded by Saudi money, would still be spouting hatred for the United States and our infidel soldiers -- especially our women soldiers – who are stationed in Islam's sacred cities of Mecca and Medina.

Finally, there would still be at least 1.3 billion Muslims living on this planet. If only one-half of 1 percent of them are Islamic extremists and jihadists, that means 6.5 million people would still be dedicating their lives to eviscerating all aspects of Western society, including but not limited to democratic rule, free speech, freedom of expression, and freedom of choice, in all its many aspects.

What would the world stand to gain? A spit of arid land that has been made tolerable, green, and productive because of the enormously inventive efforts of its citizens over the last 60 years. An end to Islamic fundamentalists' excuses that Israel is the cause of Arab poverty, illiteracy, and lack of national productivity. Of course, the possibility that these same extremists would take responsibility for their state of affairs is slim, at best. In all likelihood that honor would fall once again on the evils and pratfalls of the Western world, with the United States leading the way to hell.

So cut off aid to Israel. See what it gets the world. Bid adieu to Israeli creativity and inventiveness. There are no new ideas anymore anyway. And take Israel's soul out of the picture as well. I'm sure the rest of the world will step up and fill the holes left by the absence of the people who founded their ethics on the principles of tzedakah and tikkun olam. And if not, what's been lost? Just a little bit of light, a spark of hope, and a semblance of sanity in an otherwise bleak world.

The Fragile Circle

"We who choose to surround ourselves with lives even more temporary than our own live within a fragile circle, easily and often breached. Unable to accept its awful gaps, we still would live no other way. We cherish memory as the only certain immortality, never fully understanding the necessary plan." Irving Townsend

The quote by Irving Townsend from his book "Separate Lifetimes," is, in the context of his work, about pets, not people, the animals that came into his life and touched him for brief moments. But it's really about more than pets. It's about life.

When my wife and I moved back to Orlando in 1985 we struggled through a terrible spate of deaths. Two uncles, one great uncle, one aunt, long time family friends in the first year, and shortly thereafter, my father, and we wondered what we'd gotten into. What the hell was going on? Did someone want us to accumulate a lifetime of suffering early in our marriage? What did it all mean? Why did we have to hurt so much?

What is the plan? Is it to die first, and thus in the simplest (and hopefully least painful) way avoid the ongoing suffering that comes with loss? Or is it to tough it out, realizing that all things are temporary, all situations transient, that all we can hold onto, really, is ourselves, and the memories of all who have come before us?

The accumulation of loss is perhaps one of the few certainties we can grab hold of. As we grow older or, as a close friend of mine says, as we become "the cream rising to the top," we encounter more often, more frequently, the sad inevitability of losing everything that is most precious to us, and everyone that we love. Parents die, as do siblings and friends. Friends move away, and relationships thin.

Judaism teaches us that we bestow immortality, as Townsend says, through recollection and the memories of time together. We recall those who have passed before us by reciting the mourner's kaddish, and we name our children after those we love who are no longer with us to keep their names, their voices and faces alive. Even today my children have begun to fight over who will get to name a child after their uncle, who they loved and died so young.

Sadly, memory thins as well, and like so many things in Judaism, the thought is beautiful and sensible and rational, but we are constantly challenged to live with a sometimes bitter reality. Old pictures fade into sepia, and the voices that we held onto so dearly become more difficult to hear. Even now the sound of my father's and my brother's voices begin to mingle when I recall them, and some days I think of them often, and others not at all. It saddens me each time I realize my life goes on and they are gone, almost as if they were never here. It's this we fight as Jews, the going on without remembering what we learned, what we loved, for in forgetting our lives become more transparent, less full and disconnected, and this great conflict, between the inevitability of loss and the beautiful pain of love is the real darkness we rage against.

I am one who, for whatever reason, has always had a hard time with goodbyes, whether it's been breaking up with a girlfriend, (or being broken up with), going off to camp, sending my oldest to college or merely realizing my youngest is no longer a baby. The greater goodbyes, the permanent departures - the deaths - are so emotionally overwhelming for me that they have become almost unfathomable. I find myself surrounded by ghosts – friends lost to time, family members, and yes, even those pets that I loved and who loved me unconditionally – and their passing has made me ask myself, is memory enough? Is there anything else we can hold onto as we try to fill the empty gaps in our lives?

I could offer you the simple clichés. Love the ones you're with. Recall those who have gone with love. And I could advise you, on a deeper level, to appreciate the unique, powerful customs within which Judaism is so rich: shiva services and yarhzeits, candle lightings and prayer. But I would ask you to go a little further here, to travel with me down one of the harder paths. And that is to fill the well of memory not only with voices and names and the recollection of the good times, but to fill it with all the times, all the tears, the anger, the proud moments and the regrets, to remember by feeling the loss and the absence of all those beings, great and small, who added life to life, meaning to meaning, who gave a special significance to each day.

So what is the plan? Truthfully, we may never know. But we can fill the gaps. We can open ourselves up to the full experience, embracing the joy, the loss, the memories that form a fragile, unbreakable circle that connects us to all we ever love.

The Enemy Has A Face

Several years ago, our trip to Israel included a guest – my oldest son's best friend, a Cuban American named Chris. Chris stood out in many ways besides his last name. He had never traveled overseas before, so his passport was new and clean. He had dark hair, dark skin, and looked like, well, a friend of the family, not a member. Every time we went through Israeli security, especially at Ben Gurion airport, we had to wait for Chris, to our chagrin. He was stopped, scanned, questioned, taken to the side and finally released. We shared his discomfort at being singled out. And we knew it was the right thing to do.

Israel's security, especially at its travel hubs – airports, harbors, bus terminals – sets world standards for efficiency and success. It wasn't that Chris posed any threat. It was that he looked different, and his touch of unease combined with his Hispanic looks made him a target for Israeli profiling. Yes, profiling. Israel's security is based largely on well-trained psychological profiling that involves watching people as they move about, asking simple questions and looking into their eyes as they answer, without concern about offending anyone. Israel can do this because it isn't scared to say out loud what every other country in the world knows but whispers: all Muslims are certainly not terrorists, but virtually all terrorists are Muslims.

Just look at recent history. The Fort Hood murders carried out by Nidal Malik Hasan, an American-born Muslim, revealed the danger inherent in not recognizing psychological time bombs. And while Umar Farouk Abdulmutallab failed to blow up Northwest Flight 253 over Detroit on Christmas Day, this botched, but attempted mass murder was additional evidence (if we need any more) that an Islamist terror network, with presences everywhere in the world including the constant spewing of poison on the Internet, considers itself at war with Western civilization.

Both US Homeland Security Secretary Janet Napolitano and President Barack Obama's first reactions to the attack aboard Northwest Flight 253 were off target and make it clear how difficult it will be to change public pronouncements and political perspectives. Napolitano said that it was unconnected to a larger plot, and Obama said that Abdulmutallab appeared to be an "isolated extremist." Isolated in the sense that he acted alone, yes. Isolated in the sense that he had no connections to a global infrastructure of terrorist cells, to training and propaganda and the fomenting of hate and violence? Not at all.

Sadly, not only our leaders fail to acknowledge this obvious truth. European leaders have their heads stuck in the proverbial sand as well, and have for years. George Bush, when he was president, spoke often of a "war on terror" but he skirted the issue of identifying the enemy. And Barack Obama, while he comes close, still fails to address the key, salient point in this selfsame war on terror: that terrorists have a face. He understands that our mission is "to disrupt, to dismantle, and defeat the extremists who threaten us…anywhere where they are planning attacks…" He understands the bottom line: "Evil does exist in the world." And he is fully aware of the insidious form the enemy takes, stating that the "war" is against "a far-reaching network."

However, the paranoid fear of appearing racist, biased, of admitting that in some cases profiling makes sense, is keeping America in harm's way. We must be willing to state the obvious: the enemy has a name and a face. It is not Islam. It is radical Islam. It is a commitment by fundamentalist Muslims to a global jihad that threatens democracy, equal rights and freedom. The quandary here is that, in order to truly fight this enemy, we may have to take on an uncomfortable mantle, one that forces us to do what we don't want to do: appear racist, acknowledge the danger inherent in a select group of people, and implement security measures to account for this admission.

Armies may destabilize the terrorist networks with invading troops and smart bombs, but they won't make America safer. We have to do that ourselves by accepting the Israeli model of intelligent, transparent, in your face security.

fiftysomething

I have begun an odd adventure of sorts. Sitting at home in a down economy, doing my best to generate business where none exists, I am returning to my roots, rediscovering who I really am. And I'm doing it in an offbeat way.

It began, I suppose, with a commitment I made to myself to look back with no regrets, and if I'm to do that I have to write something more than this column. I have to write the books I've held in my mind but somehow haven't had the time or commitment or lack of excuses to actually create. So I've recommitted to my writing, and plan to have two books completed by the end of the year.

The second thing that's happened is far more strange. I've rediscovered thirtysomething, the seminal TV series from the '80s about a group of introspective (many said pretentious, self-absorbed and analytical ad nauseum) friends in their 30s trying to figure out how to make their lives make sense. The show is now being released on DVD, so I've thrown away my dusty VHS recordings (which I never rewatched), and am going through, episode by episode, reliving that time in my life when I, too, was in my 30s, newly married, wondering what my life was going to become.

Thirtysomething rubbed a lot of people the wrong way, but for me it was like watching my life unfold onscreen, better scripted, perhaps, and more compressed, but so similar it was scary. There was Michael, the Jewish ad agency exec, trying to be a good provider and loving partner to his beautiful, strong, bright, shiksa wife Hope. There were the friends, the dysfunctional Elliott who was Michael's best friend and partner in the ad agency, estranged from his wife Nancy, the mother of his two kids. And there were the singles: Gary the assistant English professor, Melissa the crazy photographer, and Ellyn the smoky-voiced, lost at love career woman. There were love affairs, deaths, failed businesses, and family traumas. I was Michael. My wife was Hope. I had those friends. I was in my thirties. We were having our first children and dealing with many of the same seemingly banal but painfully tough issues. And we were looking ahead with great dreams and anticipation. Though we didn't know what lay before us, it was all going to be better, work out, be fulfilling. We'd look back when we were in our fifties or sixties and say, "Congratulations on a job well done. Damn if we're not proud of what we accomplished."

Well, life, as we all know, doesn't run in a straight line. If there's anything we can expect, the cliché goes, it's the unexpected. If we can count on anything, it's to count on nothing working out quite the way we planned. And so, in my fifties, I find myself still in process, returning to some of the goals I laid out for myself when I was a thirtysomething. It's not that I haven't done many of the things I've wanted to do. I can look back and check off some categories. Good father. Good husband. Contributor in some form or fashion to the well-being of our community. But there are the areas I've fallen short as well, the surprises, the lost battles and failed causes, and it's those that haunt us all the most, those that, at a certain point in time, we look back on and have the aftershocks to deal with: the sadness and grief, the loss and regret, and maybe, eventually, the gratitude and relief that comes with surviving your thirties and moving on.

I had a talk with my rabbi recently. I was struggling with the concept of fate vs. free will. If, I asked him, God writes our names in the book of life during the High Holy Days, does that mean Judaism believes in fate? Or are we free to make our lives what we will? And if there's no fate, then is there no destiny, no luck, no reason to believe that being good and living good means all will end well? God, he replied, looks at us as his partners on earth. We make our lives what we will, and we manifest his good works through our own good deeds.

Fate? Destiny? No, but our duty lies in living well and doing right in this life. We don't get second chances. We make our rewards here, not in some afterlife. I knew all that, in my heart. I knew he was right. Life is what we make it, even if, in contrast to the dreams of a thirtysomething, it's never quite made according to script.

Living with Regret

Life, we all know, is a series of failures and successes, sweet and bitter moments, gains and losses that influence our moods, our sense of self, our well-being. It is a series of decisions that both take us towards and take us away, that lead us down certain paths while missing others. And with each of those decisions, unless we are blind, or shallow, or somehow able to move ahead without ever looking back, we experience some sense of regret, disappointment or dissatisfaction. Regret is a feeling of remorse for an act or failure to act. It is constantly being confronted by your bucket list, and deciding whether to go ahead and experience those dreams or accept the fact that life has interfered, that the choices you've made, whether out of necessity (making money) or fear (taking a risk) or ease (why rock the boat when things are ok?), have taken you away from what you really want to do. In general, a person who lives with regret always thinks of what he has done, and what he could have done differently.

I have come to the odd, uniquely balanced point in my life where I regret many of the things I have done, and with that knowledge, am aware of how much regret I may still experience. And of course, behind each regret is the understanding that, by acting differently, in making decisions that at the time appear "regret-free," I would have missed some of the people I love, the experiences and accomplishments that have come to define me.

Hindsight is always 20/20. It's easy to second-guess, to say what if, to replay life and in our minds do everything right. What if I'd bought Microsoft stock in 1985? What if I'd been a second later, a minute earlier? What if I'd said the right thing, or kept my mouth shut? But reality has a way of intruding. We all end up, as I have, with regrets both large and small. Some are easy to live with. Some are not. I regret the meaningless fights in old relationships. I regret not moving to LA when I was young enough to take a chance. I regret being swayed by the lure and security of easy money. But you know, I can deal with these. I can attribute them to the folly of youth, the need to provide for my family, the fear of leaping into an uncertain abyss. The regrets that haunt me, the ones that, when I dredge them up make me cringe or cry, those are the ones I can't put aside, and learning to deal with them is one of the great lessons of my life.

I regret that, when my first great dog died, she was in an emergency room instead of by my side. I regret that I was moments away when my brother died. I regret not moving my son to a more humane situation when he played baseball in high school, and watching him suffer the consequences. I regret not being wiser, more frugal, more careful with the money I've made, and having to now deal with the results during this long, hard, depression.

The question I ask, then, is not about the small regrets. It's about the big ones. And this is where I turn, where I think we all turn to our faith, our religion, to help strengthen and fortify us. What does Judaism say about dealing with the great losses and regrets of life?

There is an ancient Jewish fable told of a tiny bird and a hunter. The hunter has caught the bird for his supper, and the bird offers the hunter three pieces of wisdom in exchange for its freedom. 1. Do not seek what you cannot obtain. 2. Do not regret what you have lost. 3. Do not believe what cannot be. As the tiny bird flies away she informs the hunter that she has a pearl the size of an ostrich egg inside of her. The hunter looks up and, after a moment of regret, smiles and walks away, a little bit hungry but very much wiser.

Mark Twain said, "Twenty years from now, you will be more disappointed by the things that you didn't do than by the ones you did do..."

So this is what I'm going to do. At the very least, I'm going to peer into my bucket, and knock off some of those items I have to/want to do before it's too late. I'm going to accept the small regrets in my life as allowable mistakes, and work hard to learn from the big ones so that, when paths diverge and choices must be made, I'll be able to use the lessons of hindsight to see the way more clearly. And when that little bird of impossible remorse flies away, I'll do my best to smile, and go home to break bread with my family, built of a thousand conscious choices and loving missteps, and I'll do so, I hope, without regret.

A Good Life

When my 94 year old uncle Leon Ettinger passed away last week, it gave me pause to reflect on his life, but more than that, to reflect on a life well lived, and a gentle death, rare as it is in this era of extended care and illnesses that are managed and controlled for years longer than they once were or should be. His last few years weren't the best. His body had begun to betray him. But they weren't bad years either. He had his family around him, his children and grandchildren and great grandchildren, and they all gave him joy and peace of mind to the end.

I listened to all the stories told about his life – his love of cars and boats, his business ventures with restaurants and light bulb manufacturing plants and citrus groves, his marriage of 72 years (incredible) to my Aunt Bea. I heard that he was a strict but loving father. I heard how he lost his marbles (literally) on Miami Beach. I heard how he was a special businessman – a man of his word, a man whose handshake was the best contract you could get. And don't get me wrong. They're all good stories, warm stories, wonderful stories. But they're stories that are special, truly special, only to his family and closest friends. He didn't save thousands in a hurricane, or invent a cure for cancer or even, for that matter, citrus canker. He didn't write great books or paint great paintings (though he began to paint late in his life).

What he did right, and what he did well, was live. He lived a full life, did what he wanted, and while it sounds like, for a time, he hopped from job to job and opportunity to opportunity handed to him by his father or father-in-law, it also sounds like he did so willingly, and thoroughly enjoyed what he did, making the most of every venture, soaking them in and making them his own. And as he lived well, he died well, unburdened, without regrets, leaving behind fond memories without pain or suffering or hardship or debt. That is rare indeed.

Too often nowadays I hear different kinds of stories, see different endings between parents and their children. I hear about the parent who compromised in life, who suffered through a lifetime of work they didn't like, who stayed in a marriage that never should have been, and once it was, should have ended mercifully years ago. I witness the estranged, the lost, the parent and child no longer able or willing to communicate with one another. I listen to stories about painful, drawn out deaths from Alzheimers or cancer, and I feel for all concerned, for the elderly parent who unwillingly goes through their final debilitating years, putting their children through emotional pain and suffering along with them. I know it's the last thing they would have ever wanted to cause, but it happens again and again, and the advent of modern medicine, longer lives, makes it all the more common. I see children who have been adults for many years struggle with the medical debts, the housing issues their parents confront in old age. I watch as children grow old while their parents grow older, and sometimes this is a blessing, and sometimes a curse. In my uncle's case, it was a blessing.

He died peacefully. He left everyone well. He supported his wife in all her endeavors, and when he passed away, sad as it was, we all knew she would be all right. Different, lonelier, adjusting to a world without his presence, but all right. That is the greatest story about him that could possibly be told.

I took this summer to knock one item off my bucket list – to write something I felt I had to write. But when my Uncle Leon passed away last week, when my last living uncle became a blessed memory, he gave me a final parting gift. He helped me realize that the greatest way to live is to never have a bucket list at all. And the greatest way to die is to do so, not just at peace with yourself, but with everyone you love.

Lost And Found

Six years ago my brother tried to talk me into watching a new show on TV. He told me it was the most fascinating, cryptic, mystical show he'd ever seen, full of questions, very philosophical and thoughtful. It was about a group of people who are stranded on a mysterious island after a plane crash, and it begins with one of the crash survivors opening his eyes. The show, of course, was Lost, and I didn't listen to my brother until it had become a cultural phenomenon. At that point I was already a season behind, so I borrowed some DVDs and my wife and I spent a marathon weekend catching up and becoming Lost addicts.

Lost ended recently, and without giving much away, it would have made my brother proud. Not because it tied everything up, not because all the questions (the crux of the show) were answered, but because the themes of the show were so meaningful. All who were lost were found. There was no salvation, but there was redemption. The broken and isolated souls who inhabited the series found themselves by helping one another and accepting help from others, by becoming part of a community, by reaching out and being willing to both give and take.

The show ended with the same person, Jack, closing his eyes, and this circularity, this completeness, would have led, I know, to many conversations between me and brother Ray, who I lost nearly four years ago. I've imagined those conversations many times already. I've heard him make his points. I've imagined how I would have agreed and disagreed, how we would have laughed at something innocuous, some silly point, and how we would have compared the moments that moved us the most.

But what I've thought about the most, really, is how I would have told him that I, too, have been lost, and am on the path to being found. I would have told him that for many years I had lost my focus, my purpose, but through the hardest of times and the most difficult circumstances I have been led back, almost forced to become who I really am. I have tasted wealth and experienced power, and I have lost them, given them up, to return to my roots. I have made a circular journey back to the person I was when I got married - the writer, the dreamer, the iconoclast, and that would have made him proud. It would have made him smile broadly, and maybe shed a small tear of gratitude and relief. He would have had the brother, once again, whom he had always known.

And you have been an important part of this journey. I have been writing this column for a little longer than Lost was on the air. The style, the tone, would not have been possible without you, without the time that has passed and the experience I have gained as I have grown and grown up by writing a little more thoughtfully, thinking a little more deeply, deepening my understanding of what's really important in our community, our world, in life and love, in all those things we give up and give away, we leave on the table and pick back up again.

There are lots of unanswered questions. I still don't know where I will end up, or who, in the end, I will really be. And that's the joy of it. That's the wild ride that we're on together. What will the future hold? No one knows. And there's the mystery. There's the pathos, the bittersweet taste of striving for completion and always being a step away. We're all lost in some way. May we always strive to find ourselves, and in doing so, become who we really are.

Ashamnu

I don't know why, but every year something stands out for me during High Holy Day services. I feel connected. I'm disconnected. I beat my chest. I don't see the relevance in beating my chest. I want to stay longer. I wish I'd already left. I'm having a meaningful experience. I'm reciting prayers without thinking about them. I wonder why the person sitting across from me chose to wear that outfit. How do I keep my kippa from falling off my head?

And so it goes. One year I'm bored, the next I'm captivated. One year I can't relate to anything, the next I'm struck by the relevance of the service. A few years ago I even wrote a column about searching for meaning during the holidays and not finding it, and struck such a chord that my rabbi used it as the basis for his major sermon the following year.

This year I once again experienced something new, something unexpected, something different during my synagogue's Yom Kippur services. Maybe I'm growing up, or growing old, or just growing, but I realized as we read and repeated the Ashamnu that my reaction in the past (I haven't done any of those sins. That's not me) missed the point. I've heard it said many times, but somehow the message never sunk in until now. <u>We</u> have sinned. <u>We</u> have betrayed. <u>We</u> have stolen. <u>We</u> have corrupted. <u>We</u> have taken advantage of the weak.

We.

It almost doesn't matter what we have or haven't done. What I understood, finally, was that as I stood in services, my hand over my heart, I was taking collective responsibility for the sins of others. Whether or not I personally sinned had no bearing on my bearing witness. We rose as one, we stood as one, we prayed together because we depend on one another, because the actions of our friends, our family, our people reflect on all of us.

Why is it that we're so sensitive when a Jew is caught masterminding a pyramid scheme, or is part of a crime syndicate, or is found guilty of any heinous crime? Why do we hold Israeli soldiers more accountable for their deeds, even during times of war, than any other nation on earth does? Why are we so proud of the Nobel prize winners, the songwriters, the actors, the authors who are Jewish? Why? Because they are all reflections of us. They are who we are, and we are part of them.

Maybe it struck me this year because we are all feeling the impact of the times. Maybe it's because we need each other more, because we're hurting more, because the synagogue is one of the few places that offers unreserved support for us all. Maybe it's because I looked around during services and felt that I was being taken care of by others, and that in turn I was taking care of them. I was carrying some of their weight, their burdens as they carried mine. We lifted one another. We held each other up in a collective gesture of forgiveness and grace.

We are Bernie Madoff. And we are Elie Wiesel.

We are Mickey Cohen. And we are Albert Einstein.

We are Michael Milken. And we are Louis Brandeis.

We are every Jew who has caused pain, and every Jew who has saved a life, and we carry the burden, and the blessing of both.

Maybe that's what makes us a people. It's not cultural. It's not 4,000+ years of shared history (though it's both of those as well). It's because we think of We, not I. As Jews it is not you and me. It is us. Together, good and bad, light and dark. We are a shared collective of accountability for our behavior, our actions, for all the results of who we are. That's something I can beat my chest about.

2011

Metal Sculpture

The Hungry Season

A friend of mine told me a story recently, a true story about a client of his. I don't know this client, whether the person being discussed is male or female, old or young, but it doesn't really matter. Let's assume he's male, and for the purposes of this tale we'll call him Mr. Owner.

Now Mr. Owner owns a construction company here in Central Florida, and as everyone who owns a business knows, the past few years have been tough, so tough that people like Mr. Owner have been bidding low, extremely low on new jobs, just to keep their doors open and their employees occupied. Mr. Owner was lucky enough to land a million dollar construction job, and like any good businessperson would, he negotiated the heck out of all the vendors and sub-contractors who worked for him. Guys who were used to being project managers were working as field superintendents. Field superintendents were working in the field. Men in the field who were used to making \$25/hour were sucking it up and making \$10/hour. Why? Because that's all there was out there, and something, anything, was better than nothing. Because then they at least had a chance to put food on the table and keep the lights on for wife and kids.

This wasn't a huge job, but at the time it was Mr. Owner's only job, so he was out at the work site quite a bit, and one day during the lunch break he heard the workers, his "subs," laughing and joking, and he wanted to know what they were laughing about. They told him that after lunch every day they threw their wrappers and scraps into the nearby dumpster, and every night someone, (they assumed it was some poor, homeless person) crawled into the dumpster and ate whatever food they hadn't consumed. Cold leftover French fries. Bits of burgers. Whatever they left this person ate. And they thought it was the funniest thing ever. The image of this someone picking through the trash every night cracked them up.

Mr. Owner listened, and he was shocked, then angry, and finally irate. "You should be ashamed of yourselves," he said. "This isn't funny at all. Whoever is doing this is obviously desperate and starving or they wouldn't be picking through your waste." He thought for a minute, and then he said, "And this is what you're going to do. Starting right now you're going to go out every day and buy this person a meal. And not just any meal, but a good hot meal from some place like Chili's or Boston Market. You're going to leave it by the dumpster every night, and every morning you're going to put the receipt on my desk. I don't care if you draw straws or take turns or how you work the rotation of who's buying the meal. But it's going to happen every day. And the first day I don't get a receipt you're all fired. I can replace you in a heartbeat. There are hundreds of people clamoring to do your jobs. And I want to see vegetables on the receipts, not burgers and fries!"

And from that day forward every day the workers on the construction site bought a good meal for the hungry stranger and left it by the dumpster. And every morning when they checked the meal was gone. This went on for about a month, until one day the workers went to see Mr. Owner.

They were concerned. More than concerned, they were frightened because for the past week the meals had gone untouched. They didn't know what had happened to the person they'd fed. Was he/she dead? Had they simply gone somewhere else? Were they in jail, hurt, sick? They desperately wanted to know so they could help, but they never found out, and no other meals they bought were ever eaten again.

This true story doesn't have a happy ending. Like so much of life, it simply trailed off into a grey area of uncertainty, hope tainted with doubt and despair. But it amazes me nonetheless.

Why?

Because the workers here were all transformed, not because they knew the person they fed, not because they heard a story of need that touched their hearts, but through the very act of giving they came to care. They invested themselves in the well-being of someone else, and because of that their cruel laughter turned into genuine concern.

What is the moral of the story? That giving changes everyone it touches, from the one who receives aid to the one who provides it. And the change is deep, and positive, ultimately working on a soul level.

And that can change the world.

In this new season of hope and fresh starts, may we all experience the joy of generosity and be transformed by the power of giving.

Freedom At What Cost

I feel guilty even as I begin to write. The joy and relief felt by Jews worldwide at the release of Gilad Shalit from five years of captivity at the hands of Hamas is real, deep, and deservedly so. How many times have our rabbis asked us to think about and pray for him since his capture? How often have we wondered if he, like so many other Israeli soldiers, was being tortured by terrorists, and if his life was already forfeit? To the Shalit family, we all say thank God your son has been returned. But his release came at a high cost.

Just as Israeli leadership looked into the eyes of Gilad's parents and vowed that he would someday be freed, so too they look today into the eyes of hundreds of other parents whose children were murdered by militant Islamic terrorists and say, "We're sorry." For while there can be no doubt that saving Gilad Shalit was a great ending to a horrific story, the epilogue is, at best, bittersweet. More than 500 Arab prisoners have to date been freed in the exchange for Gilad, including convicted terrorists and murderers, and this is where I cringe. This is the bile on which I choke. Israel swore it would never release prisoners with blood on their hands, and now it has.

It's not up to me to question the internal decision making of the Israeli government. Nor do I want to diminish the accomplishment of freeing an Israeli soldier, or the value of his life. But I do want to remember the eyes and thoughts and feelings of those other parents who lost children and now must live with the murderers going free. It is those people who I don't want to diminish either, for I know how I would feel if I were either parent – the one whose children was lost, and the one whose child was returned.

Freed were:

Yehiyah Sinwar, a founder of Hamas' military wing, who had served almost 25 years of four life sentences he was given for his role in the abduction and killing of two Israeli soldiers in the 1980s. Showing no remorse, he immediately called on the capture of more Israeli soldiers to help free thousands of other Palestinians in Israeli jails.

Wafa al-Biss, a 26-year-old woman who was arrested in 2004 for trying to detonate explosives strapped to her body at an Israeli checkpoint near Gaza. "We shall continue on this path of struggle and resistance and martyrdom," al-Biss said Wednesday evening.

The woman who drove the car for the bomber of the Sbarro pizza restaurant in 2001, and was closely involved in the planning of the attack that murdered 15 people and injured 130, is being released. Again showing no remorse, she declared that she knew she'd be let out in a prisoner swap at some point, and when set free, she'd carry on. When asked on television whether she knew how many children had been killed in that attack, she replied that she did not. On being told that the number was eight, she smiled for the camera.

Dalia Cohen's daughter Kinneret was murdered in 1989 by terrorist Abed al-Hadi Ganaim when he took control of a public bus and drove it off a cliff.

"On the one hand, I am happy that Gilad is coming back to his mother," says Dalia. "I am also a mother and I know what it's like. I know how much I would want to get my child back. Everybody is happy around me but I cannot rejoice. Abed al-Hadi Ganaim was set free today. I feel like I am betraying my daughter. I feel like she is screaming, her blood, her ashes are crying out to us and I cannot do anything to prevent it."

According to a 2007 report by an Israeli terrorism victims group, 177 Israelis were murdered in the five years before the study by recidivist terrorists who had been freed.

Abbas ibn Muhammad Alsayd, released in 1996, was subsequently involved in three terrorist attacks, including the 2002 bombing of a Netanya Passover Seder. In 1998, Iyad Sawalha was released as a "good-will" gesture; in 2002 he detonated a bomb that killed 17. And in 2003, Ramez Sali Abu Salmin was released; 7 months later he blew himself up in a Jerusalem cafe, killing 7.

Being a Jew is a complicated enterprise. On the one hand, we value each individual life as sacred, and maintain our morals and our sense of justice and righteousness and integrity as if our lives, rather than our reputations, depended on it. On the other hand we live in a world of greys, a harsh, pragmatic world of dealmakers and compromise, and the very values we live for are often undermined for the sake of a clearly mixed good. We are complex. We are conflicted. We are, in our hearts, trying our best. But even the best intentions are often challenged by a bitter dose of reality. I am happy for Gilad and his family. I am sad and dismayed for the families whose children died at the hands of now free murderers, and I am scared of what the future may bring.

The Joy of New Beginnings

A funny thing happened to me and my wife recently. She decided to finally fill in some of the blanks on her Facebook page, and entered her relationship status as "married to David Bornstein." She had no idea that in doing so she was actually updating her personal information, which meant that Facebook automatically sent out a message to everyone to whom she was connected announcing her marriage. Our son texted in his congratulations. Our daughter called us weirdos. I told everyone that she finally said yes. Numerous friends commented that a marriage isn't official nowadays until it's confirmed on Facebook. I laughed and enjoyed all the responses. And I thought to myself that on a deeper level, something else was going on.

The truth is, while the Facebook announcement didn't really mark a change in our marriage status of 26 years, there are a lot of changes in our personal lives we could have announced in Facebook but haven't. New jobs. A new home address. Children starting new schools, going away to school, and with that our family dynamics changing in ways we've thought about for years. But now what was far away is here, and there's no going back. Our lives will never be the same again.

I've spoken to a number of couples who are new empty nesters, their only child or last child gone away at last to college. And while there's always a coming back, there's never a coming back for good. And while there are always wistful thoughts and painfully sweet memories and equally painful regrets, to a person everyone I've spoken to has been remarkably upbeat and happy. Their schedules have been freed up. The house is quieter. It's not a mess. The kid's rooms aren't disaster areas. There's a sense of peace and calm that permeates through the walls. They're all glad to be starting the next phase of their lives.

And there are many others here in Central Florida who find themselves beginning again. The newly divorced who are looking forward to finding a rewarding love – the right love this time. The flotsam and jetsam victims of the economy who are reinventing themselves, starting new businesses, creating new niches that just may be a better fit. The recent college graduates who, instead of choosing the easy path and moving back in with Mom and Dad have decided to work a year for low pay at a job that they've always dreamed about. The student who struggled in college and took time off only to go back recommitted, focused, with outcomes in mind and goals to achieve. The couple who, their children gone and their homes empty, find time to hold hands, take walks, rediscover themselves and all the reasons they're together.

Even as I write this I realize that today was my brother's birthday, and that in the five years since his death so much has changed in my life, so much has emptied out, but now it's being refilled. His death left a huge hole for me, and yet, even that hole had a bottom, a light at the top, a way out. We've begun again in so many ways, rebuilt, added to our lives, and yes, announced our marriage on Facebook.

And in a sense, isn't that what this time of the year is all about? My brother's birth and death both occurred around Rosh Hashana, our time of new beginnings, and as I mark his life I also mark mine by celebrating a new year.

Little Tyrants, Big Issues

Every game this fall the head coach of my son Gabriel's little league team has picked a different boy to be team captain. That boy gets to set the starting lineup, making up the batting order and placing kids at their positions in the field. Invariably, with the exception of two boys, the captain has placed himself in the field at a position of prime importance, and batted third or fourth, the top two hitting spots in the order. I've been frustrated as I've watched. Does every kid think they're the best hitter on the team? Is there no hope for putting the team first, before the individual? Have these ten and eleven year olds already been indoctrinated in the "me first" system of values that seems so endemic in our society? Are they already little tyrants who can't see past the tips of their own noses?

Sadly, I believe the answer is yes. Most of these boys, at a very young age, are already protecting their self-interests to the detriment of the greater good. And on a larger, far more magnified scale, we see it in our society as well.

I have been pondering the enormous moral implications, not of baseball lineups, but of the horrific case of years of child abuse charged against Penn State assistant coach Jerry Sandusky, and the downfall of football coach Joe Paterno and university president Graham Spanier in its aftermath. Paterno, the winningest coach in college football history and head coach at Penn State for more than 40 years, was an institution unto himself. I have to admit I have thought for a long time that his best coaching days were a decade behind him, but I also thought that as a man of high moral values he deserved a great deal of positive acclaim. He gave and raised millions of dollars for higher education. He raised the profile of Penn State enormously. And, until his inglorious ending, his record for a clean and dignified program was beyond reproach.

Sometime around 2002 Paterno reported Sandusky's disgusting moral terpitude to his superiors, and nothing was done. I can imagine the back door conversations that took place. "Thanks, Joe. We'll take it from here. Please don't say anything about this to anyone. It would only bring scandal and disgrace to the university, and we don't want that to happen. We'll deal with things." And Paterno probably washed his hands of the matter at that point, relieved that he'd done his duty, unwilling at the same time to take on his bosses and become the snitch, the whistleblower, the tattler against his best friend – even if it meant other children might be harmed.

But no one ever did anything. Sandusky remained employed. And Paterno didn't do what many now say he should have done: gotten rid of Sandusky, his close friend, and taken the case to the next level. For Paterno, his fault was not in doing something wrong, but in not doing enough, and this lapse of judgment cost him his job and, in all likelihood, his reputation. Why? Because he lost sight of what was really important, what was the overriding wrong – the abuse of helpless boys. Instead, he focused on his world, his fiefdom – college football, and this shortsighted desire to continue to run the Penn State program led to his ultimate demise.

Part of this is cultural. We've all let certain institutions like college sports become too big, to the point where they overshadow our basic human values. Part of this is our own drive for self-promotion and self preservation. And no one is questioning Paterno's integrity. He proved that time and again over a long and distinguished career. But questions abound now about his moral courage. And that is the toughest, highest hill we all must face and climb someday. It's not about doing what's right with the simple issues in life. It's not about putting yourself lower in the batting order, a simple task that Gabriel's teammates consistently failed at. It's about doing what's right when there's tremendous risk.

Think for a moment about our own focus on the righteous gentiles of World War II. Jeopardizing their safety and the lives of their families, a handful of people laid everything on the line to save Jewish lives. But thousands more, many living in the shadows of the concentration camps, did nothing at all. And I have to ask myself, if I were faced with the same dilemma, while I know what I would want to do, would I have the moral courage to do it? Would I endanger myself and my family to save the lives of others, hundreds, even thousands of others? Or in the case of Joe Paterno, a few young boys? Would I? I don't know.

We come across self-motivated little tyrants in every day life, again and again. The boss who makes himself look good while hurting others. The spoiled athlete who sacrifices team goals for personal accolades and statistics. The millionaire who says he can't afford to help the poor as he returns from a vacation in Europe. The people who stick their heads in the sand and say, "We didn't see anything."

Our challenge, when faced with the truly difficult decision, is to climb the hill, to take a stand beyond personal integrity and reach for the heights of real moral courage, to go the extra mile and do what's right, oftentimes regardless of the consequences.

Take it from the examples of the righteous gentiles. Take it from the two boys who put the team before themselves and chose to bat low in the order. It may be the hardest act a human being can do. It may also be, in certain circumstances, in those situations that define us for eternity, the only righteous act there is.

House

It's just a house. Walls and roofs. A place to eat, sleep and store stuff – the accumulated stuff of a lifetime. To a builder it's a product. Build it, maybe live in it awhile and move on. To others it's no more than a stage in life. Ten years here. Then ten years there. Change addresses and lifestyles to meet the needs of a changing family.

But sometimes it's more.

Sometimes it's your heart and soul. Sometimes it becomes part of your family. Sometimes it's the realization of a dream. Sometimes it's the reward of the long road you've traveled.

My parents built one house in their entire time together. I grew up in downtown Orlando, at 244 Whittier Circle. I still remember our phone number from that house, and my images of childhood all are wrapped around those rooms, that neighborhood, summers swimming in that deep pool, the Florida room with terrazzo floors and a walk-in closet full of toys, Shabbat dinners in that dining room around the oval, dark wood table, the hiding places inside the cupboards down the long hallway with the high, narrow windows. That's my map of memories, and when I recall, in thought or dream, my earliest years, that's what comes to mind.

My wife and I have just signed a contract to sell our house, the one we built together to raise our children, the one that may be the only one we ever build, as it was for my parents. We moved from downtown Orlando when we needed another bedroom for our third child, and we chose Maitland to be near the hub and core of the Jewish community. Together we selected every item, from faucets to light fixtures to countertops to the style of toilets to the size and configuration of the rooms. And then we added more, built-ins and furniture customized by our tastes to fit our house. A decade has passed.

Our youngest, Gabriel, now eleven, has known only this house. He loves it, and he's a little scared, and very sad about saying farewell. All his childhood memories will be about this singular place, filled with the colors of his bedroom, his bookshelves lined with his prized possessions, his recollections of our Shabbat dinners around our round kitchen table, playing with his friends in the cul-de-sac at the end of our street. These will be the residual images of his past. Now we are moving on, and our goal, our duty, our responsibility to him is to make another home.

It's not easy, giving up a dream, even when you know it's the right thing to do. Financially it makes sense. And downsizing, from the grand house we built to a more manageable, maintainable one for only three full-time inhabitants is the right choice. It comes with the territory. It's part of the deal when your family shrinks and children move on. But it still feels like giving up a lot, like saying goodbye, not to something, but to someone who has nurtured and protected us, who is filled with the essence of us, who holds in their being all the key components of what has made us a family. That will soon be gone, and we'll be making a new start in a new place with events that will not be shared by all of us but only by three of five. That will be different.

We've found a smaller house in a good family neighborhood, and I realize, as I admonish myself, that lots of people have less. Lots of people are worse off and we're really fine. Even so, the other day I dropped Gabriel off at school and as I drove past our house and pulled into the driveway I grew wistful, nostalgic, and began my own process of parting and putting this decade in the life of my family in my pocket, on a shelf, there but set aside to reflect on as we move on to other houses, other lives.

HOUSE

House that has only known us
House built with the sweat of frustration
And bricks of memory

And footers of family dinners
And the beams of childhood
And the cracks of parenting
And the settling of middle age

House that has felt the anger of youth
Holes punched in drywall
Walls smeared with the afterthoughts of circus and fair
Floors scuffed with puddles of thunderous play
And witnessed the hidden joy of first sex
And young love
And long settled love
House that has watched the progress
Of a marriage both difficult and profound
Turn gentle slow and tender
House that has seen blood shed
Food burnt
Doors opened and lights left on
House that has been entered and left
Countless times
Driven by countless times
Sheltered us through hurricane and recession
Cradled us in safety even as we shouted obscenities
Screamed in pain
Denied the truth
Decried our fate
House that never abandoned us
Now we prepare to abandon you

May the next family live as long
Be as happy and sad
Feel the full range of joy and anger
Disappointment and fulfillment
Experience the pride of making a place their own
Home
As we did all these years.

The Jewish Path

We are almost empty nesters. Our oldest son and daughter are now both away at college, and we are left with Gabriel, our 11 year old. There may be more to write about that someday – the new only child, the next phase of life – but this is about my daughter, and what she has experienced so far as a freshman at the University of Georgia.

I've realized, in my daily conversations with her, that there is much to be proud of, and many things I wish I'd done as a parent before she left home. She's bright, determined, capable, independent – all qualities we want our children to have by the time they leave home. She's eager for new experiences, interested in learning all the things she doesn't know and exploring a part of the world that's different than where she grew up. And that's all very good.

Of course, as she's asked me questions about auto maintenance, schedule management, and even postage and shipping options for packages, I've realized there were things left undone. I should have had her change a car tire. I should have taken her with me to the post office, to a hardware store, so she would have firsthand understanding of some life skills I take for granted. And perhaps I should have explained to her that, when she moves away from home, she'll run into more people with values that are different than ours, disturbing, perhaps, bewildering and inexplicable. I could have told her to expect to deal with hatred, jealousy, and yes, anti-semitism. I'm not sure she would have believed me then. I think she does now, at least a little bit.

Her plan all along was to go to UGA a week early to rush, to try to get in to a sorority. The way she figured it, it would be a fun way to meet other girls even if she decided not to join, and if she liked a sorority and joined one, all the better. Her social life would suddenly be full.

The week of rushing quickly became intense. Up every morning at 5:30, breakfast at 6, then a rigorous schedule that included touring 17 different houses, meeting dozens and dozens of girls, and trying to stand out in a crowd of 1,200 who wanted to be special enough to be selected by the sorority of their choice. She was warned. Most girls did not get an offer from their top selection. But she was hopeful nonetheless. Her biggest concern going in was that she wanted to be in a sorority other than the one for Jewish girls.

It wasn't a self-hating sort of deal. She likes being Jewish. She went to the Hebrew Day School. She'd just finished a summer of being a counselor at the JCC. She just didn't want to be labeled. She didn't want a stereotype tagged to her in her new environs right away. And yes, there was probably some fear about being stuck in a group of bright, geeky, unpopular Jewish girls.

Her initial interviews went well. She felt good about them. So did her roommate, a sweet Georgia girl with a thick southern accent who is devoutly Christian. But when the offers came back, her roommate got a bunch, including her top choice, and Jerica got three. She got the sense, upon reflection, that many of the sororities wrote her off right away. She didn't think it had anything to do with how she presented herself. But she had a sense that it could have had something to do with her last name, or possibly the belief, on the part of the interviewers, that she would automatically choose, or be better off at, the Jewish sorority. She couldn't pinpoint this. There was no proof, nothing explicitly said. It was just a feeling she had, but it made her sad. She felt like she wasn't even given a chance to show them who she was, because (maybe) she was Jewish.

And then something amazing started to happen. She listened to her heart and came to realize that, out of all the girls she'd met, out of all the talks she'd had and places she'd visited, the Jewish sorority was one of her favorites. The girls were really chill. They were fun, and smart, and sweet, and pretty.

Out of every sorority, it had on its own become one of her top two selections, and they had also selected her. By the end of the week she'd done a complete 180, and happily, gladly joined Sigma Delta Tau. And she's been abundantly happy with her choice ever since.

In her first weeks away from home, my daughter learned some of the most important lessons of her life, more important than changing a tire or mailing a package. She learned that some people are so different from her that they may not get her, that they may be stuck in their own preconceptions, and that in our modern world this may be unclear, uncertain, but it may still be present. And she learned that by following her heart she could find a path that was clear, make a decision that felt right, and in doing so be truer to herself than ever before.

The Second Wife

My wife Pat and I were at a little league game recently, watching our youngest play. Now lest anyone think this is just another baseball column, don't worry. You're safe. We sat in the first row of the bleachers where we had a clear view of the entire field, huddled close, as is our way, taking the opportunity to catch up on a long week of missing each other. We exchanged news of the day. We held hands and kissed, not passionately, but as a sign of affection, a way to reconnect.

Standing behind us were two pretty young moms, one African American, one blonde, chatting away about being single parents. I overheard snippets of their conversation, one talking about how close she was to changing her marital status, the other all about her son, who was, as she described, bright and sensitive and struggling on the field. Our son Gabriel took his last at-bat, and Pat asked if it would be all right for her to leave a little bit early to go home and settle in. I nodded, and she took off as the loudspeakers blared "Blinded By The Night."

The blonde, the mother with the sensitive boy, started talking about the song. "Does anyone know the words?" she said. "We've all been singing this since we were in high school and no one knows what they're saying." Good point, I thought, and I proceeded to look up the lyrics on my iPhone. "Blinded by the light, revved up like a deuce, another runner in the night. " I passed my phone back to her. She looked at the words, then asked, "Which boy is yours?"

"The little lefty in center field," I responded.

"Is that your stepson?" she inquired matter of factly.

I blinked, jerked back my head. I didn't understand. "My what? No, that's my son."

"Oh, I'm sorry," she stammered, "I just assumed, the way you two were acting, that was your second wife."

"My second wife?" I shook my head again. "Nope. 26 years. One happy marriage."

"Sorry," she said. "I guess I assumed wrong."

We didn't say another word to each other, but I laughed inside, then thought for a long time about what she said. My second wife. Was it because we still snuggled, because we were still happy, caring, gentle in our mannerisms? Was it because Pat looks so much younger than me (7 years separate us)? Or something else? And then I had a different thought entirely. What is it about us that makes snap judgments about someone else? Was she reacting out of her own singleness, or because of our behavior, or was there something in her past that triggered her reaction?

In Malcolm Gladwell's book "Blink" he goes into great detail about the instant decisions people make, and how we can trust and evaluate them. And whole fields of psychology are devoted to our immediate likes or dislikes of people when we first meet them, before we even know anything about them. This person is cold, this one off-putting, this one could be my best friend. But the truth is, none of these snapshot perceptions are based on reality. They are based, in large part, on material we carry within ourselves. And that material often writes whole scenarios for us before they ever occur. False scenarios. Shallow scenarios.

Judaism teaches us something different. It reminds us over and over, again and again, that who we are, that what defines us and everyone around us, is not the false perception, or the gossip and rumor, or the charm or the looks. It is our actions. It is what we do and how we live and thus, our split second reactions to others ought necessarily be tempered by time and experience. That is how we truly know the depths and merits of the individual. That, perhaps, is what the blonde single mom misread between me and Pat – a love that has deepened and strengthened and matured over the years, not the flirty, cooing, bat your eyes romance she imagined was the second marriage.

And so I laughed, and reflected, and when I went home and walked in the door to our house and saw my beautiful bride of 26 years, I greeted her by saying, "Hello second wife."

"You have a story to tell me," she responded.

Battle Hymn Of A Jewish Tiger Dad

I have to admit, I don't get all the fuss about the Chinese tiger mom. What's wrong with her? She knows who she is, and so do I. I am strong. I am powerful. I am confident (even if my wife calls me gefilte breath first thing every morning). Inside, I know. I am (with her permission) Jewish tiger dad.

I've been a Jewish tiger dad since my first child was born. No, make that since before he was born. Five hours of piano a day? Pheh! He was listening to Mozart 24/7 IN THE WOMB! When my wife gave birth I fully expected him to come out singing hallelujah and reciting algorithms. So it took a few more years. Like the jungle predator waiting for his prey in the tall grass, Jewish tiger dads understand patience.

I, too, have called my children garbage. Well, maybe nice garbage, because they're sensitive and I wouldn't want to hurt their feelings. And really, maybe not garbage, but I've commented from time to time that they're a little messy and they need to clean their rooms before I do. But then they're so busy with their self-improvement projects (learning to speed text, Facebook social negotiations, keeping up with important reality TV trends), that I go ahead and clean their rooms for them.

Control their schedules? Do I ever control their schedules! No playing after school. Religious school twice a week like any good Jewish child. No sleepovers (except with their grandmother, and when, upon closer examination, they convince me that it is vital for their behavioral development). And then of course my oldest is such a jock how can I deny him what he does best, so I let him play sports after school and miss religious school once in awhile. However, I make sure I am there at all times, micromanaging like any good Jewish tiger dad would. And my daughter has perfected such a demanding whine. Oy! How did she ever learn that the one weakness a Jewish tiger dad has is to his daughter's constant whine. If I let her visit with her friends when she finishes her homework, and talk undisturbed on her cell phone, will the world end? I think not. And my littlest, with those baby blue eyes, well, he gets an immediate dispensation for being so sweet and beautiful.

High standards. I have set the highest standards for my children. Nothing but straight A's in school. If someone does better on a test, more studying! Work harder! I oversee them for ten minutes, fifteen minutes, twenty minutes, their tiny hands clutching hard wooden pencils, one math problem after another being completed, and I watch the callouses grow on their fingers, and the pencil slips in their sweaty, shaking hands. What's a Jewish tiger dad to do? I make the tough decision. I give them a break and a cup of chocolate milk to reward them for their hard work.

My youngest goes out and buys me a birthday card, and I throw it back in his face. "It's not good enough for me," I tell him. "I deserve better. The joke in the inside didn't make me laugh. You call that a punch line? I'll show you a punch line." And then I hug him and tell him I'm only joking because I worry that he might almost be crying.

I threaten to take away my daughter's laptop and donate it to our synagogue if she cannot master her haftorah in six weeks. When she masters her haftorah I threaten to take away her afternoon snack and her manicure appointments for the next two or three months (tops, I promise her) if she cannot do a little bit more of the service. When she learns more of the service I say to myself, "Hah! I am a great Jewish tiger dad."

There are things that go wrong, as they do in anyone's life. My children scream that I am too hard on them, unfair, that I occasionally don't think of them first. A hamster dies and I must deal with loss and grief and the possibility that I didn't make them clean the hamster's cage often enough. This is a failing I know I must confront, and I do so with the steely resolve of a wild animal. They start driving and manage to disable the GPS tracking devices I've installed in their cars and don't answer their cell phones every time I call (not more than twice in any given hour, I guarantee you). But these are the trials the Jewish tiger dad faces, and I persevere.

And now the most difficult challenge approaches as my children, my cubs, leave home and depart for college. I must deal with the fact that my job is done, their training is over, and they must confront the world on their own. But then, I realize, there is still hope. Given the economy today 80% of all college graduates move back in with their parents, and I realize I have not been put to pasture yet. The Jewish tiger dad will live to hunt another day!

2012

Clare on the beach

Searching For Clare

Out of nowhere, I've had two related dreams recently, both having to do with one of the great loves of my life. No, they weren't about my children, or my wife, but about a dog.

In many ways, Clare was more than a dog. She was my once in a lifetime dog. I bought her for $20 at the University of Michigan bookstore. I was second in line for her, and the cashier selling her told me to come back and if the guy who said he wanted her didn't show, she was mine. Luckily, amazingly, he never did. She was a small ball of black fluff, a mix of Newfoundland, Labrador, and Golden Retriever, and as she and I grew up together, me into adulthood and she through her life, we formed a bond that for me was unique, unrepeatable, almost psychic in its depth.

She learned commands without me teaching them. I never had to put her on a leash. She knew to wait at street corners, to come whenever she was called, to stay by my side when we took long walks. I never had to worry about where she was, because she was always right there beside me. She was my companion through my lonely days between relationships, through my marriage, the death of my father, the birth of my first child. She had the incredible propensity, on our long daily walks, to find food wherever we went - discarded pizza, bagels, hamburgers, cupcakes - and she'd want to eat them desperately, to scarf them down before I knew what she was doing. But she also felt so guilty about eating what she knew wasn't allowed that she would sidle right up to me with her mouth stuffed full of whatever she'd found, looking up at me with her big brown eyes, begging me not to look down. But I always saw. I always knew what she was up to, and I'd tell her "Drop it!" and she would, wagging her tail happily when she realized she'd done right by me.

Two of the biggest regrets of my life have to do with Clare as well, and when I think of them they still make me cry.

The first, that once when she was an old dog and Ethan, our first child, was a baby, she was barking while he napped, and I smacked her under the jaw to quiet her without warning. The second, that I wasn't there when she died. She had cancer and was in the emergency vet clinic, and even though I woke at 5:30 a.m., bolting out of bed as if I'd had a premonition to get her early, I was too late, and she passed away without me next to her.

Both dreams have had to do with me finding her again, or her finding me, and I've wondered what they've meant, since each time they've been haunting, emotional, unsettling. And I've come to realize that the dreams are about Clare…and they're not. On a deeper level they've been about my personal search for connection and meaning, for wanting more of those few real moments in life that can only be called epiphanies, moments that are at once happy, peaceful, fulfilling and filled with an understanding that can't be put into words.

I've had a few of those moments in my life. Standing on a mountain top after a hard day of hiking and looking across three mountain ranges into clear blue sky. The births of each of my three children. Watching my wife sleeping next to me and realizing she is mine and I am hers for the rest of our lives. Catching a falling leaf on a chilly autumn day and for a second getting leaf, tree, and wind. Standing and sitting at shul and feeling the rhythm of prayer and community as they rise and fall together with me wrapped in their healing arms. And yes, there were moments with Clare, playing, walking together, realizing how short her life would be compared to mine, how I would never have another one like her again.

And isn't that what we're really here for? Not the mundane, repeated daily patterns that blend together without distinguishing themselves. Not the ordinary, everyday occurrences, but the extraordinary, the rare moments when we find ourselves connected to something higher, something better, brighter, something (dare I say it?) approaching divine. Those are the moments I am searching for, the dreams that keep pushing me forward, the vision of the possibility of life's best moments, like the ones I had with Clare.

The Swinging Door

This morning I fixed the bathroom door, the louvered one that swings open and closed and blocks the toilet from public view. We thought it was busted. For the past few weeks it wasn't swinging shut all the way, stuck halfway open and halfway closed, and I was preparing to take it off its hinges so I could replace the broken parts at our local hardware store. I got a Philips screwdriver and, lying on my back, looking up at what I thought was a cracked piece of plastic, I noticed a screw was missing. One tiny screw that attached the door to an L-shaped brace had somehow disappeared, and that was causing the door to remain open when it should have swung shut on its own. I went out to the garage, got a screw and fixed the door. Now it closes perfectly, with ease.

We'd been living with the door like that for weeks and weeks because I hadn't gotten down on the floor and looked closely at what was going on. Once I saw the hole where the screw went, the solution was obvious, the problem solved.

All I had to do was stop for a moment and take a closer look.

So many of the moments that seem like epiphanies in my life are just that: moments when I've stopped for the briefest of instances and taken a closer look, a second look. When I think about the images I often recall as those when time stopped, when I knew I was witness to something important, something transcendent, it was only because I had taken the time to notice. It wasn't time that had stopped. I had.

A driveway in Ann Arbor made of pebbles, that led to a house that led to a door that opened to....I never knew, but I'll always remember a path, a door, an opening to something new.

Hiking hard, driven by thirst, I stop for a moment to look out over worn, green mountains, a crystal blue sky stark in its stillness behind them. A moment of such beauty, such tranquility, as tired and thirsty as I was I'll never forget it.

Sitting with my brother in his darkened living room while he remained motionless on the couch, eyes closed, head tilted back, recovering from his last bout of chemotherapy, and realizing I was already being told goodbye.

Watching my youngest come out of our synagogue after Sunday school one morning, his yarmulke still on his head, and realizing this was it, the last one, a bar mitzvah, a few years of high school and then they would all be gone and our lives would, not start again, but move in a different direction.

The quiet and stillness of each of these moments will stay with me forever, and maybe that's the lesson here. It's an old cliché, a tired truism about stopping to smell the flowers, to take time to see what's right in front of us, but there's something to be said about noticing, not just the grains of sand that fall through your hands, but the grain that catches your eye. There's a reason that meditation is so calming and attractive, why quiet is necessary, why the Zen concept of living in the now is so appealing. It's because so many of those moments pass us by, flit away without us being aware of them at all.

Maybe it's not about living life to the fullest, but living life to the smallest. Maybe it's both. Maybe it's the acknowledgement that there are instances in life that are special - minor encapsulated miracles that only require our attention to bloom into wonder, insight, epiphany. Maybe it's as simple as looking up at a door hinge, or down, past the tips of our noses, so we can see what's been in front of us all along.

Simple Acts Of Faith

In the winter of 1974 my friend Gene from Brandeis University visited me during the winter break. I was a college sophomore, and the times were very different. I had a big Jew-fro, the citrus industry in Central Florida was still almost as important as tourism and Disney, and the world seemed full of promise and possibility.

One afternoon, looking for something to do, Gene and I went out to our family's orange grove in Polk County adjacent to the Green Swamp. We brought a package of bottle rockets with us, figuring it would be fun to shoot them off into the swamp. Let's just say our senses were heightened that day, our moods excellent. It was cold and windy, but we were determined, and persevered with our mission. We stood at the edge of the swamp, poised between orange trees and wilderness, waited until the wind died down, and lit the first rocket. It flew into the air, and as soon as it exploded the wind howled again. Hmm, we thought. Interesting coincidence. We set off another rocket and the same thing happened. The air was quiet, but as soon as the rocket blew up, so did the wind, gusting and screeching. We tested it. We waited a few minutes while the wind died down, then did it again, and again. And each time the wind rose exactly in time with our exploding rockets. It was amazing, miraculous, coincidental perhaps, but it seemed magical to us, as if a higher power were present.

Just recently I sold a pair of shoes I wasn't wearing on eBay. The buyer lived in Alaska, and I shipped them off to the address he provided. It turned out to be an old address, and he never received the shoes. We had a friendly back and forth about this. I offered to reimburse him. He politely refused, chalking it up to strange karma. And then a month later the shoes appeared back on my doorstep, and I got in touch with him, got the correct address, shipped the shoes off and offered to split the postage with him. He paid the full amount. A small gesture on both our parts, but one that reaffirmed my faith, at least, in the kindness and generosity of strangers.

And this past year, after struggling through the recession to maintain loans on two properties, after working with my bank through numerous issues, after carrying the properties long after I should, we reached an amicable solution to the business deals and my wife and I were released from our guarantees and allowed to move forward with our lives. I know many people who have fought with banks, struggled with loans, been adversarial and hurt in the process. I tried to be open and honest, and for once, it paid off. This all concluded on Erev Rosh Hashana. Coincidence? Maybe. But it was definitely another confirmation, for me, that good deeds are actually, sometimes rewarded.

Many of us have had incidents like these in our lives - positive moments that reestablish our faith in goodness, semi-mystical moments that bring the wonder and mystery of the universe into direct contact with our consciousness, inexplicable moments that seem to sprout from some divine source. I don't feel unique or special in having these happen to me. What I do feel is a strong desire to recognize and acknowledge these moments when they occur. Sometimes it's just serendipity, the random coming together of innocuous events that end up having special meaning. Sometimes it seems like more.

I have long struggled with many of the basic tenets of faith. Is there a God? Do our lives really have meaning beyond the day-to-day humdrum of existence? Is there such a thing as fate, or destiny, or a spark of the divine anywhere at all? What comes next? And for the most part, my answers fall in shades of grey. I don't know, and most of the time I'm at peace with that. But then there are bottle rockets, and lost shoes, and honorable people in business, and I find my faith in something more affirmed, and life quiets and takes on a sheen that lightens my footsteps and gives me, briefly, in the smallest way, a gentle inner glow.

My Mother Who Lives Alone

A few weeks ago my mother missed her reading group. Within a few hours alarms were raised. Friend called friend. I got a call from my aunt and cousin, both of whom were concerned about her safety and wellbeing. I had my own full schedule to keep, and a daughter who was driving home on her own for spring break from Athens, Georgia, so I was already anxious and a little strung out. Finally, with no answer on either her home or cell phone, my wife and I drove to her house, imagining best and worst case scenarios. Best case: we find her watching TV in her bedroom, oblivious to the panic going on around her. Worst case….I don't want to think about the worst case.

Of course, neither came to pass. As we pulled into my mother's driveway she was right in front of us, and we spoke to her in the garage. She explained what had happened that morning. She went to the wrong house because the normal meeting place had been changed, unbeknownst to her. She got lost. She called some, but not all of the people in her group. I was too distraught to do anything but show my angst and frustration, and so we left with a "We're glad you're all right," and nothing more. An hour later she called me to tell me how angry she was that I hadn't reacted with more concern for her, that I hadn't kissed her hello or good-bye, that I had chastised instead of been effusive with relief. And the truth is, I wasn't compassionate. I was stressed. And that is the problem.

My mother. Fiery, bright, active and independent to a fault. She moves too fast for her own good. She's opinionated and tough, and she's also generous, caring, understanding and has shown an amazing capacity for growth for a woman approaching 87. That being said, she is also a perfect example of what many of us face – parents growing older, and with their age the need for additional help, new limits and restrictions while at the same time (and this is the catch) maintaining their sense of self-dignity and freedom. It's a difficult, near impossible balancing act, especially with someone like my mother who keeps her hands busy and my hands full.

You see, every time I call her house and she doesn't answer, I worry. If a few days go by and I don't hear from her, I worry. When she calls me at odd hours of the night, I don't just worry, I momentarily panic, until she tells me she's trying to remember the date of the Entebbe raid, or something like that. Is that reason enough to insist that she give up what she perceives as the definition of her independence – her living by herself and taking care of herself? Probably not. Is the time coming when her need for additional care may mandate a move? Possibly. Most assisted living facilities won't take in an already infirmed senior, so the move has to be made while she's well. But does my peace of mind supersede her desire to live alone, and her disdain, for whatever reason, of apartment-style senior housing? Not yet. But at some point it will.

I can tell how cautious she is about what she tells me, about how she eats, how she drives, how well she's doing in general. She's scared of my forming the opinion that now is the time to make a move, that I'm going to push her into selling her home, and so I see her act warily around me on occasion, and I don't want that, either. What I want is for her to be well, to be happy, to live in her old age as she wants. But I don't want her or anyone else getting hurt in the process.

When do you tell your parent they can no longer drive? When do you worry that they've lost too much weight? When do you say enough, it's time to acknowledge the limitations of your age? It's a high wire my mother and I walk together, and the fear is falling without a safety net, and the reality is that getting old isn't easy, but neither is watching your parent grow old while you stand helplessly by.

My Grandfather's Nose

My grandfather had a world-class nose. Not just a stupendous schnozz, or a big nose, but a wide, imposing nose that spanned his face like the Golden Gate Bridge spans San Francisco Bay. That wasn't his only outstanding feature, just his most prominent one. His ears stuck out from his head like flaps on a jet. I imagined he used them to slow himself down when he was running too fast, and if he drove a convertible, they probably caused him to get worse gas mileage. He had a bald, bulbous head that would have been perfectly polished were it not for the three or four wild hairs that always sprouted up in just such a way that they caught the light and thus, my attention. But it was his nose that stood out. I could never get past his nose.

It had been broken several times during his childhood in czarist Russia, hit by rocks thrown at the Jewish ghetto kids by neighborhood boys, and was never fixed properly. And so it stretched out across his face, making him both look and sound like no one else I ever knew.

You see, his voice was affected by his nose as well. Nasally just begins to describe it. Think of a bassoon rumbling up through bellows into an ancient megaphone. That was the sound of my grandfather's voice. And when he sang it became amplified, rumbling, even more nasally, like a back-of-the-throat duck call.

He lived with us from the time I was six and my brother was four. He'd been injured in a fire, and while he recuperated in the bedroom next to us, with his legs smelling like overcooked, smoked meat, our parents added a room to the house and his infirmary became his bedroom. It wasn't bad having him in the house. In fact, it was nice growing up with three generations under one roof. He went out to restaurants with us, offering to pay for the meal when the total cost for the family was below $25, and he still drove out to work every morning to check on the small orange grove he owned, though I wouldn't be caught dead in the same car. For him, driving was always about how few times he'd swerve over the center line, not if. He mostly stayed in his room, watching The Lawrence Welk Show, Perry Mason, and Petticoat Junction, but he joined us for every dinner, and he led the blessings every Friday night for Shabbat.

My brother and I suffered through the Sabbath prayers. We came to the dinner table hungry, ready to sit down for our 20 minute family dinner and eat eat eat like the ravenous cannibal boys we were. Waiting for the blessings to be done was torture. The prayers over the bread, the wine, the Sabbath day all took so interminably long, and our grandfather droned on and on, stretching out the vowels, warbling through the melody as only his cavernous nostrils could.

Most of the time we held it together. But once, we just couldn't. We didn't mean any disrespect. We were just boys, and something struck us as funny. Maybe it was the waiting, or the sound of his voice, or his seriousness compared to our irreverence. I looked over at Ray. He raised his eyebrows, a smile breaking across his face. I started to giggle. So did he. Our grandfather paused, looked over at us, and continued, the cup of wine held in his hand, vibrating with each syllable sung. Ray started to laugh. This was funnier and funnier. The whole room seemed to vibrate with the singing, the chairs, the table, I could even feel it inside my stomach, in my head, my eardrums throbbing with the sonorous chanting. I saw our sister nudge Ray. He covered his mouth with his hand. This made it all even more hilarious to me. I burst out laughing.

"David," my father said, "stop being so disrespectful."

"I can't," I told him, tears in my eyes.

When Ray heard this he burst out in laughter and ran out of the dining room.

"What's gotten into them?" my mother said to the table. My grandfather stood there, still and dumbfounded, waiting for a signal to continue. That's when I lost control, opening my mouth and exploding with laughter like a container under too much pressure. I ran out of the room, too, found Ray in our bedroom and fell on the floor with him, our knees weak with what we both thought was the most comical situation we'd ever experienced. We didn't know why. It just was.

After a few minutes we stood back up and returned, knowing that the only way we could worm ourselves back into our parents and grandfather's good graces was to look as contrite as possible. I knew what to do and say, and as soon as I re-entered I said, "I'm sorry, Grandpa. I don't know why I was laughing."

Until this point Ray was right there with me, head bowed down, eyes to the ground, looking like the whipped dogs we were trying to emulate, but he couldn't help himself.

"Thanks for the best Shabbat ever, Grandpa," he said. "Let's do it this way every week."

Was it the best? Maybe not, but it was definitely one of the most fun and joyous. And unbeknownst to my grandfather, it was a gift, because ever since, when I think of him and remember family Shabbat, I have no choice. All I can do is smile.

Who Loves Israel More?

I have avoided writing anything political during this heated, overblown, obscenely expensive presidential election because, honestly, I'm no more a political expert than the next person. All I have are my opinions, like anyone else, and my biases. However, as a Jew who cares deeply about Israel I have listened with great interest to what both candidates have espoused over the past year, and in President Obama's case, watched what he's done over the past four years, and I've come to a rather startling conclusion: this year, there is no issue regarding Israel.

Listen to me carefully, especially all of you one-issue voters who put Israel above the environment, taxes, the economy, women's rights, civil rights, wars elsewhere in the world, and every other topic I can think of: there is no Israel issue this year.

What brought me to this conclusion? Simple. The constant one-upmanship between the two candidates over who loves Israel more. Governor Romney states unequivocally that he is a friend of Israel. President Obama (whether you believe it or not) has proven, through his actions over the past four years, that he is a staunch supporter of Israel. He made sure there was funding for the Iron Dome missile defense program. He has spent more time with Netanyahu than with any other world leader. So let's take them both at face value.

I imagine a conversation between the two candidates regarding their support for Israel sounding something like this:
Mitt: I love Israel.
Barack: Well I love Israel more.
Mitt: I love Israel more than the world.
Barack: I love Israel more than the world times infinity.
Mitt: Benjamin's my best friend.

Barack: Well I call him Benny and he has my special phone number so he can call me any time, day or night.

Mitt: When I'm president I'll give him my cell phone number. So there.

Barack: When Benny calls me I speak to him in Hebrew.

Mitt: I speak in Hebrew and Yiddush.

Barack: I speak in Hebrew and Yiddush and gave Benny my secret military decoder ring.

Mitt: I keep kosher.

Barack: I'm planning to convert.

Mitt: I can't convert but my best friend's Jewish.

Barack: Michelle's parents may be Ethiopian Jews.

Mitt: Well Jesus was Jewish.

Barack: Oy vey.

The point is, both will support Israel. Neither will abandon Israel. Nor will the world end, the ten plagues be revisited, or there be any need to move to Canada or Costa Rica regardless of who wins. The United States will not go socialist if Obama wins a second term. As far as I can tell, we haven't done so in his first term. And by the way, he's not Muslim. Nor will we return to the dark ages under the leadership of Romney. Those emotional, extremist positions have no place in this election as it becomes more and more centrist. And this leads me to another simple conclusion: if you can't hang your vote on the Israel issue, because both men are ardent supporters of the state, you have to look at the other issues and decide. And those issues are many and critical.

There is one question I'd like to leave you with about the Middle East. It's not about who will give Israel more military aid, or who will work to stop Iran from going nuclear. I believe both men will, and both men must. It's about the long-term safety and security of Israel that will only come with a peaceful resolution to the longstanding conflict, and the real question is, which man offers a greater chance to negotiate, or at the very least lay the groundwork for negotiating, a peaceful solution, one that includes, as it inevitably must, a Palestinian state and safe borders for Israel? Which man can best lead that process further down the path towards final acceptance? That is the question you should be asking yourself before you vote.

I'm not going to advise you how to vote. I'm only going to ask you to vote. Florida is one of the pivotal swing states, and your vote matters. Rather, let's hear it for the end of political ads on TV, unanswered questions in debates, petulant posturing and the "I Love Israel More" contest.

Control

I have spent the past several months helping my mother transition into a new living situation, and with it has come an enormous paring down of her possessions. Now I'll say up front that she's been great about it – decisive, smart, willing to part with many things she held onto for years. And her taste and style – impeccable. But oh the partings, and the volume! Let's just say that she, like many others who have lived a long life, collected a great deal while sorting through and throwing away very little. Her high heels could have provided enough spikes to lay train tracks cross-country. And her purses, in every size, shape, color and material imaginable, could have outfitted all the fashionistas of Park Avenue, if not all of Central Florida.

There was order and organization to her stockpile, arranged as it was by color and fabric. And I took lessons from her organizational acumen, so that when the women in our family went through the shoes and purses and outfits that my mother had accumulated and now let go, there would be a semblance of orderliness and control. I wanted to make sure the ransacking....I mean the distribution....was fair, that no one got hurt, no one took advantage, no one got more or less than their fair share. For whatever reason, this was extremely important to me. So I drew names from a hat, created a list so the women would pick in order. Front to back. Back to front. Everyone would have the same number of chances to pick what they wanted. I would be their chaperone, casting firm decisions when there was conflict, making sure everything went according to plan. There was some minor dissention, but I knew it was for the best. I'd heard too many horror stories about families at each other's throats during these trying times of property distribution.

What happened?

Chaos! My list was ignored. There was no orderly line, no taking turns, no thought given to who got what, or how much, or when or why or how come. They waded into the mass of purses, ignoring any semblance of sense, and had at it, grabbing, inspecting, dropping one, shuffling through and picking up something else. And what was the result?

Perfection.

To a person, the women in my family – my wife, sister, daughter, niece, and soon to be niece-in-law, helped one another sort through the mass of purses to find the best ones for each of them. They were generous, kind, took only what made sense, gave away what suited someone else better, and their tastes and styles were so different they each came away content, having enjoyed the process and shared a great time together – despite me, despite all the order and control I tried to impose.

What did I learn? What meaning did I glean from all of this? First, I don't know if my attempt at order and control helped, but maybe it did. Maybe there needed to be the thought of order, a beginning based on control for such a mass level of love and compassion to rule. Maybe, because the rules were there in the first place, when they fell apart the intent of the rule remained. And of course – maybe not.

Maybe sometimes we don't need control. Maybe giving up control and letting life take over makes more sense. Maybe we have to simply trust our own good nature, and allow it to roll forward, and hope it will all come out all right in the end.

As Jews we know that life isn't always that kind, that understanding. There is justice and injustice. There are acts of great human charity, and unspeakable acts of inhumanity that make no sense, will never make sense, for as long as history is written and remembered. As Jews we live with the threat of communal extinction, the fear of personal dissolution and assimilation every day we live. Israel is threatened on all sides. We are attacked as a people, misunderstood as individuals, misrepresented in the press, maligned in world courts, and making sense of this, imposing order on what makes so little logic is an enormous, draining struggle.

So this coming calendar year I'm proposing something preposterous, something profoundly different. Let's try giving up a bit of the control we've held onto so precariously, as if it were a precious commodity. Maybe if we forgot the rules of the Middle East and just talked something would come of it. Maybe if we listened. Maybe if we looked across the imaginary borders we've constructed that separate us and realized that we can give, and share, and love even though our tastes and styles are completely different, maybe the world would change a little. Maybe I'm just being naïve, but then again, maybe not.

Reconnecting With Genius

Those of you who know me personally know that I (along with 10,000 other people every year) graduated from The University of Michigan. It's where I received both my undergraduate and graduate degrees, and where I met my wife. That was a long time ago, but what you may not know is that before Michigan I went to Brandeis University for two years. Little Brandeis in Waltham, Massachusetts. Jewish Brandeis, where if you're not a Jew from the northeast, you're a minority. Exceptional Brandeis – one of the finest colleges in the country.

I didn't last long there. I was young, having skipped my senior year of high school to go to college, and got very little input from anyone regarding my choice of schools. I didn't realize Brandeis was so small, so Jewish, that I would feel like so much of the school had no bearing on me. I wasn't interested in taking classes on any aspect of Judaism or social work (the two mainstays of the curriculum), and since I also wouldn't take a class that started before 10 a.m. I found my choices severely limited. But I did one thing right while I was there. I made great friends.

There was red-haired Rob, a roommate for one semester, and tall, long-haired Don, who became a judge, and Eric, who brought his Irish Setter to school and later became a doctor, and Scott, who all the girls loved and today is an Ayurvedic physician. And there was Gene, who played classical piano and was kind and gentle and non-judgmental and, I discovered at some point, gay. Gene and I became close friends. Platonic, mind you, without there ever being any issues regarding his sexuality, or mine. We were open-minded, supportive, good friends. We had some amazing experiences together. And we haven't been in touch in 30 years.

Somehow, my last semester at Brandeis I landed a single bedroom in the dorms, and my room was right above Eric and Gene's. I'd walk downstairs to hang out with them, and Gene often came up to chill with me. After I transferred to Michigan, I visited my friends there once, and saw Gene and Eric and Scott in NYC, and Gene visited me both in Ann Arbor and Orlando. But that was all many years ago. And then, for some unknown reason, we lost touch. It wasn't because anything happened. We just faded out of each other's lives.

Once, about five years ago, I made a halfhearted effort to get in touch with Gene. I contacted the Alumni Association at Brandeis and got nowhere, and honestly, I dropped the ball pretty quickly. I didn't push, didn't really try. But I've been thinking a lot lately about all the people who have disappeared in my life, friends who have moved away and lost touch, loved ones who have died, friendships that were important for a time, for a reason, a season, but have since ended. And I found myself thinking about Gene.

Out of all the friends I made at Brandeis, he was the one who was the most accepting, the most supportive, the one who I felt cared about me the most, and the one who, out of everyone, I regretted losing the most. So I contacted the Alumni Association again, but this time I got somewhere. They gave me his last known address, and I googled him and found him in San Francisco, and last week we connected via email, and yesterday we spoke for the first time in three decades. It was in an email that he reminded me that I called him Genius, and that touched my heart, and when I sent him pictures of my family he wistfully remembered my long, black, curly hair, and I reminded him that all things pass away – our looks, our friends, our lives.

Still, it was amazing to reconnect. We spoke for more than an hour, and caught up as best we could. I told Gene about all the ups and downs of my life, and the good path I'm on now, and he relayed the same. His parents moved from Brooklyn to Delray Beach, so he comes to Florida often. He's HIV+, which I thought was a possibility, but he's healthy and doesn't have full-blown AIDS. He's single, and searching, and his heart is wide open, as it always was. And what was great for me was that I found something that I thought was lost forever, a true friend who is now back in my life, and I've realized that while everything does change, while nothing stays the same, while life does ebb and peak and slip through hands like water, it also sometimes flows back in miraculous ways.

In Dog We Trust

Everyone knows there are dog people and cat people (and people who don't care about animals at all, but I'm not going to talk about them). Cat people tend to be attracted to the independent, laissez-faire attitude of felines. You clean their litter box, sit on your couch and, if your cat deigns to grace you with its presence, it will leap into your lap for a few minutes of purring and stroking before it decides to jump off and do what it wants again. Cats come and go. Their minds are their own. And this appeals to a certain type of person.

Dog people, on the other hand, tend to crave what dogs offer. Unlimited, non-judgmental love and loyalty. Free kisses and tail wagging. Warm welcomes always. Trainability combined with an eager to please attitude. Dog people love the emotional reciprocal connection they have with their pets. And dogs... well, a good dog is the embodiment of love. It's no wonder dog is god spelled backwards.

While I've had cats my whole life and loved and enjoyed them, I am a dog person through and through. So are both my oldest and youngest sons. We are dog whisperers. We feel the connection, understand the needs, empathize with the hurts and sense the minor inconsistencies that foretell illness or wounds. And when we don't have a dog, life has a hole that can't be filled, an emptiness that won't go away until a pooch is in our arms.

Growing up, I was a lonely child. I had one best friend who was a year older than me, and when he went to junior high school he dropped me like a rock. I looked in corners and hidden places for a replacement. I begged my parents to let me have an iguana, imagining if I had a lizard sitting on my shoulder I would feel less alone. I got the iguana, but I was wrong. I talked them into letting me have a little squirrel monkey I named Chatter, but I never spent the time I should with it, and when I did it sat on my shoulders, but bit my ears mercilessly, and when it died I was both sad and relieved.

It wasn't until years later, when I was in college and found my dream dog, Clare (whom I have written about) that I felt the old dark space I carried for so long disappear. And when she died after nearly 14 great years, I wondered if I would ever have a dog like her again.

Twice in one lifetime, I knew, was too much to ask. I brought home a poorly bred Newfoundland puppy who died of a heart condition at age 4, and a beautiful flat-coated retriever named Chloe after that who came close to perfection, but she died of cancer at 8 and never had the chance to live her fullest. Then we moved, and were petless, and my youngest son Gabriel yearned for a dog of his own. For a year and a half the mantra of our house was "I need a dog." He made a Power Point presentation about how much he needed a dog. He twisted every conversation around to "That's because I need a dog." And we said no. And we waited. And he wondered if it would ever happen, if he would ever feel that unrestrained love that only a puppy can give.

And then, this past summer, acting in my typically compulsive way, I began scanning pet rescue sites. We weren't committed to being overly righteous. I suppose if a perfect purebred dog fell in our laps we would have said yes. But it didn't, and we liked the idea of starting a relationship by saving a puppy.

Somehow, for some reason I still don't know, one morning I searched for mastiffs and three labrador/mastiff mixes popped up in a Tennessee shelter. It was the first day they were listed online, and I called and they were still available. I showed my wife, who inexplicably said, "It feels right," and we made a donation, selected a pup named Rosa and made arrangements to pick her up when we took Gabriel to summer camp.

As it turns out, as fate and the stars would have it, the shelter gave Rosa away, and saved one of the other puppies for us, and she has turned out to be... well, perfect describes her perfectly. Sweet, smart, non-destructive – we call her our new dogter. Best of all, Gabriel loves her as much as she loves him. His mantra has changed from "I need a dog" to "I have a dog" and "I love my dog." He has found the fulfillment only a boy and his dog understand. And I am so happy for him.

Sadly, like so many things in life, dogs exist for a moment, not a lifetime. They are with us briefly, and as much as seeing Gabriel and our puppy together makes me smile and laugh, I also understand how rare these great loves are, how often we wish for them, how long we wait for them, how quickly they disappear. Judaism teaches us to put the needs of our animals -livestock and pets – before our own. And it teaches us (though phrased differently) to love one another as we want to be loved. What better example of this can there be than the love of a boy and his dog?

We are a new family now, an expanded family with a white-socked, tail wagging, tongue flopping new member who wakes us every morning like it's the first day of the universe, with joy and gratitude and lots of kisses. God keeps teaching me how to live, but dogs have taught me and my children how to love.

2013

Torah reading

The Youngest Bar Mitzvah

There are some moments in life you imagine long before they occur. The birth of your first child, and seeing him or her for the first time. The death of a parent and what you'll say, how you'll feel to truly be without the safety net they always provided, even in their old age. Saying goodbye to your children when they go to college. Trying to decide what to do with yourself when you're an empty nester for the first time after a lifetime of caring for your chicks.

There's a moment that I've thought about for a dozen years that's none of these. It's the bar mitzvah of my third and youngest child. Gabriel is nearly seven years younger than his sister, ten years younger than his brother. The gap in time makes the impact of the event, for me, even more powerful. He is the baby, the last, and I know now, having been through it twice before, that the years from bar/bat mitzvah to high school graduation and college telescope. They move at a faster, almost blinding speed, compressing time and making it difficult to hold onto memories, to hold onto the child for a few more years while letting them go to become adults.

I've imagined both my older son and daughter coming home from wherever they are in school for the bar mitzvah weekend. I've imagined us all sitting in the first row of our sanctuary, staring up at Gabriel as he chants his Torah portion and haftorah. I've wondered what his speech will be like, the obligatory thank yous and jokes about his siblings or parents. And I've seen, in my mind, the expression on my face, a mixture of sadness and joy and pride as I begin the process of a final goodbye.

I've learned a few things, having been through the b'nai mitzvah circuit twice. I've learned that it isn't necessary to have the fanciest invitation or the biggest party or the most lavish kiddush luncheon to make an event meaningful and special. I've learned it's easy to go overboard with any and all of these, and that, for the most part, kids don't care. They want to have a good time with their friends and the family members they love most. Everything else is superfluous. We've made our share of mistakes, and I'm sure we'll make some more. But most importantly, I've learned that the focus ought to be on Gabriel and not on anything else – on the meaning he gets from the weekend, on the charitable work he does leading up to it, on the choices he makes regarding a tallit, an invitation, a party.

Gabriel is proof that predictions and projections by parents are worthless, a waste of time. As much as I've seen the future in my mind's eye, I've washed it clean as we approach his bar mitzvah. He is, he wants to be, his own person, and to date, as much as any twelve year old can, he's succeeded. With my oldest son I learned the hard way that living vicariously though your child's accomplishments comes at a heavy cost, often the burden of major regrets and embarrassments. With my daughter I learned how to say yes and no, how to provide empathy and support when she needs it most, how to stand firm when she needs to learn to stand on her own. And with Gabriel I've learned the joy in letting him be Gabriel.

I always imagined I'd have a serious, studious child with curly black hair, a semi-goth who loved to read late at night and write overwrought poems and walk around pretending to be Keats or Shelley or Eliot. But that was me, and it has been none of my children. And while Gabriel is like me in many ways – irreverent to a fault, creative in unexpected ways – he's also funnier than me, more out of the box than me, more honest with himself and open with his feelings than I am, even now at age 56. He plays trumpet and tennis. He's obsessed with his puppy. He is challenged but not intimidated by the opposite sex. He's centered and solid and very, very unique.

Gabriel has taught me and keeps teaching me to wipe the slate clean, to look into the future but to put no credence in any of it, because he's creating it as he goes, and it's nothing I could imagine or expect. My older children will come home for the weekend, and we will sit in the front row and kvell. But everything else is up to G. And so we begin this last bar mitzvah season together, the youngest leading his old man into new territory, and my eyes are open wide, and every moment going forward is gift wrapped with surprise.

The Girlfriend's Dilemma

The girlfriend had been living with her boyfriend for nearly seven years. They lived a good life. He owned a successful business he'd built up himself. She worked at a highly respected international environmental organization. She was extremely cool – bright, funny, well liked by all. Neither were young anymore. They'd both been married once, and though they loved one another, hadn't yet gotten over the bad taste their previous, difficult relationships had left. So, while they didn't rule out tying the knot someday, they weren't in any hurry to head back to the altar.

There were many reasons for this besides the failed first marriages. He had two college age children. The daughter was still in college. The son was more of a free spirit who worked part-time for his dad, went to community college a bit, lived with them and was making a name for himself as one of the premier DJs in the area.

She had no children. Nor had she been around to help raise her boyfriend's. By the time they were involved the children were young adults. This led to several problematic issues.

Since she was the live-in girlfriend, the two children deigned to listen to her as they would any adult, but not as their parent. The daughter breezed in and out of the townhouse they lived in as she saw fit, often with friends from school. She largely took care of herself, worked hard in school and in the summer, and caused no one any difficulties.

The son...well, the son was another story. It's not that he was a bad kid. Not close. Big-hearted, happy, good-looking. He didn't have a malicious bone in his body. He just didn't have a plan. Girls loved him. He worked enough to get by. His gigs kept him out at the oddest hours, and he'd traipse in sometime between 2 a.m. and the time he had to show up for work at his dad's place.

This all concerned the girlfriend. It created an air of instability in the house, and she often felt as if she was a distant last place to everyone else. Her boyfriend put his children's needs first, even though they were old enough to be on their own. The crazy hours the son kept, the different girls coming and going....the girlfriend could only hope he'd had the right conversations with his dad about everything from STDs to prophylactics. Because she couldn't tell him anything. Even though they liked one another, she was more a big sister than a mom. And because of all this, even though she loved her boyfriend, she was thinking of moving out and getting a place of her own.

So when the son started stirring early one morning the girlfriend knew something was up. And when he walked to the stairwell and looked down at her, she wondered what he was going to say. And when he yelled, "Hey R-----, do you know how much the morning after pill costs?" she nearly choked on her breakfast.

A million thoughts went through her mind at once. A million questions. What's been going on upstairs? Doesn't he know better? Does he know anything? Has his dad ever talked to him about sex? Should I? I just want to scream at him. Didn't he use a condom? What girl was up there last night anyway? Is she still here? Were there more than one? If I say how much the pill costs will he think his dad got me pregnant and I took it? If I say I don't know will I sound like an idiot? I can't deal with this before work. It's even before my first cup of coffee.

Just then, luckily, thankfully, the sister, who was home on vacation called out, "$20!" and he said, "Thanks" and went back into his bedroom to sleep.

The girlfriend was left dumbfounded.

What she thought, for a moment as she drank her coffee, picked up her keys, her pocketbook and headed out the door, was "I'm not his parent. I should never be put in this situation in the first place. I have to move out."

But then she thought again, and she realized something. He had asked her. He had opened his door and asked her, maybe flippantly, maybe in the spur of the moment, a personal, important question. A question that exposed himself to her. In a way, he was saying, "I need help. I need your advice. I made a mistake, and I acknowledge that you're the adult around here."

Sure, she was bailed out by little sis. But she was also included in the family circle. And so she decided to stay, and the son eventually got his own place, and while they're not necessarily living happily ever after, they're a whole lot closer to it.

This year, may we all find ourselves in the right place, surrounded by the ones we love.

When Enough Is Enough

When my mother moved into her new home, I did two simple things to make her life easier: I picked up her mail at her old address, and I had her phone calls from her old phone number forwarded to me, so I could direct them appropriately.

Now, I'm sure you're thinking, picking up the mail makes sense. It's a nice favor any good son would do for his mother. But having her phone calls forwarded to me? Why not simply have them forwarded to her? The reason, you see, is that for years she had complained about how many solicitations she received daily over the phone. Being the doubting son I am, I assumed she exaggerated. It couldn't possibly be the six or ten calls a day she swore she answered. More likely one or two that made it feel like the phone was ringing non-stop.

Well, it was.

I currently receive a half-dozen calls or more a day on my cell phone, from unknown numbers, from places as far away as the state of Washington, from places I know no one like Mississippi, all asking for contributions.

But that's not where it ends. Somewhere along the way she made a contribution to some organization that labeled her an easy ask, and that organization forwarded her name and address (yes, and phone number if they had it) to every other obscure charitable organization in existence.

How obscure, you ask? Some of them aren't, since they include every Jewish organization in Central Florida. But others are, shall we say, remarkably specific. One week's worth of mail included the following (and this is only a partial list): The Poetry Foundation, Florida Opera Theater, The Smile Train, Earthjustice, Memorial Sloan-Kettering Cancer Center, The Foundation for AIDS Research, Lambda Legal, The National

Trust for Historic Preservation, Defenders of Wildlife, Waterkeeper Alliance, The National Museum of the American Indian, National Parks Conservation Association, Noam Shabbos, Simon Wiesenthal Center, Human Rights Campaign, St. Joseph's Indian School, Doctors Without Borders, Parkinson's Disease Foundation, Easter Seals, Mothers Against Drunk Driving, Leukemia Lymphoma Society, Southern Poverty Law Center, Public Citizen, Weizmann Institute of Science, Alzheimer's Disease Research, Macular Degeneration Research, Feeding America, American Society for Yad Vashem, Prevent Blindness America, Boys Town, The AARP, The Environmental Defense Fund, First Step (whatever that is), and of course the ASPCA.

Now lest you think my mother is merely a bleeding heart liberal who gave to every needy left wing organization, she was also on the list of the Democratic National Committee and the Republican Party of Florida.

I have come up with a pat answer to every phone call, a reply to every mailing: my mother has given enough. She is well into her 80s, has lived a life of generosity and charitable giving, and now it's time to give her a break.

Judaism teaches us, of course, to heal the world – tikkun olam – and I was brought up with that as one of my family's core values. And I was taught both by my faith and my parents that giving back is central to being a good person. The quandary I faced, then, was how did I take that away from someone who has given all her life, when she defines herself, in part, by how much she gives, even if it's ten dollars to the Southern Poverty Law Center?

What I've told my mother is twofold. First, that she's given enough, that she has consistently given when called upon, even when I have pleaded with her to scale back, and that now she can look at the accumulated philanthropy of a lifetime and rest on her laurels. She has supported every organization that has needed help, and now it's time, finally, to help herself.

But there's another part of the message, and it is l'dor va dor, that there must be generational continuity as well. It can't always be our elders who carry the load. The principles and philosophy of charity must be passed on and the mantle taken up by the next generation and the next. And when it is our turn, and our children's turn, our parents and our children's grandparents can truly know they have passed on enduring values that enrich lives. And that's when it's ok to say dayenu. Enough. I've healed what I can. Now it's my children's turn to take up the call.

The Year Of Understanding

Many, many years ago a dear friend sent me a story in the mail. This was before the advent of email or text messages. It was old style, hard copy, stapled and folded and sent in an envelope. She worked in New York City at the Atlantic Monthly. My wife and I had moved to Orlando, so the gap was great, and where we had once carpooled together to work in Detroit, now we talked occasionally and saw one another less and less frequently. Today we are barely in touch at all, but for some reason I recently found the story in a pile of old writing materials and read it for the first time.

The story, by Ethan Canin, is called "The Year of Getting to Know Us," and in the top right hand corner she wrote a note. "What a pleasure – love, Ani." What a pleasure, I read, and so I plunged in, expecting a good read, and a pleasurable one, a gentle romance, a thoughtful memoir, a bittersweet coming of age story. What I got, instead, was a well-written, tough story about a father and son – a father who can't love, who is obsessed with golf to the detriment of his family, who is having an affair and no longer loves his wife, finally abandoning her and his son, his only child. And now he is dying and his son is trying to make sense of things – who he is, what his father's connection to him is, and why he can't express his emotions, love in particular. When I was done I put the story down, turned to my wife, described it and asked, "Why did Ani say that was a pleasure? I'd call it many things, but pleasure isn't one of them."

I've sent her an email and asked her that question. But in the meantime I've asked it of myself. Was it a pleasure? What did I get out of it? And why was I so struck by her tiny, handwritten comment?

The easy answer is that I was taken aback, surprised by an outcome that didn't meet my expectations. But that is superficial at best. The real answer, I think as I delve a little deeper, is that the short story was pleasurable, just in a way that I was unprepared for, because the pleasure I got out of it was born out of the pain of understanding who my parents and I really are.

Now I'm not going to go into details here. Those are best kept private, as some secrets and stories should be known only within closed family circles. What I will say is that it relates as much, if not more, to me than it does to either my mother or father, because one of the last building blocks of maturity finally comes when you start to see yourself as clearly as you see them – the warts, the failures, the flaws as well as the achievements and successes we so ardently express. I listen to the praise of my own children, their own inflated sense of who I am, how much I know and am capable of, and wonder what it will be like for them when, in their eyes, I fall back down to earth.

I know it has been a challenge for me, for in seeing my parents' limitations I must admit my own. And as I write I look around and see drawings of me done by family and friends, their own interpretation of who I was, and I know I am all of those things and none of those things, dust and dreams and figments of the imagination, and they are gone from me, separated from me, lost to time and distance as I am left with who I am – someone who has tried to be successful, to do good, to live up to his personal goals and dreams, succeeding occasionally, failing as often as not.

Every year we are asked and expected to light yahrzeit candles for family who have passed away, to create light to remember them by. My father's death, occurring as it did on my birthday, is now a time when I look at myself as well as remember him, and both pictures are filled with holes and cracks. And as I patch the holes and seal the cracks I think perhaps I understand a bit of what Ani meant, without meaning to, about the unspoken pleasure, painful as it is, of coming to terms with a deeper understanding.

Meditations On Mother

When I was a junior in high school, I decided to skip my senior year and go straight to college. No one questioned my decision. Everyone thought I knew best for myself, in large part because the world perceived me as a really smart kid. Which was true, up to a point. I was also unsure, unclear, with no path before me and no real idea who I was.

So I applied to college, without anyone advising me where to go or what to look for. Harvard told me to wait a year. Amherst and Yale turned me down directly. The University of Florida begged me to come and offered me a full academic scholarship. Instead, I chose the best university I got into – Brandeis University.

I didn't know what I wanted to study, what I wanted to do with my life. I thought I might be a writer, maybe a lawyer like my dad. But really, I had no clue. I didn't identify with being Jewish, nor did any of my friends (though we all were). I had no idea that the school I was going to was 90% Jewish, barely larger than my high school, that I would be considered a minority because I was a southern Jew, and not from New York or New Jersey. I'd never officially visited, never taken a tour, didn't know what I was getting myself into.

At Brandeis I tried on every façade I could, anything other than something Jewish. At my roommate's recommendation I started playing saxophone, but I'm no musician. I called myself a writer, but I'd written very little of a serious nature, and didn't get into the one writing class I applied to that required writing samples for admission. I tried smoking a pipe (the tobacco kind, in this case), wore tweed jackets, had a massive Jew-fro, pretended to be worldly and sophisticated even though I wasn't even close.

As a freshman I lived in the old Ridgewood dorms, cranky, dilapidated two-story buildings with spacious double occupancy rooms on the first floor and tiny singles and double occupancy rooms on the second. I, of course, was in one of the cramped upstairs rooms with a piano-playing roommate named Steve Wininger who chain-smoked and always seemed to have girls sleeping with him, which meant I had to find somewhere else to go. Most of the time I hunkered down with my two buddies below me, Eric and Gene. And we were all under the watchful, if slightly off-kilter eyes of our residence advisor, Rick, who lived in the single next to me.

Rick believed, rightly or wrongly, that everyone should do as he did. He was a black belt in karate, so he thought everyone should take karate. And he was into transcendental meditation, so he thought everyone should learn TM.

TM had just exploded in popularity across the country, and the Maharishi Mahesh Yogi was making his first trip to the United States. As part of the celebration, the big TM center in Copley Square had a special introductory offer going on. Rick talked us into going. Eric and Gene went first and started meditating twice a day, twenty minutes each time. Steve and I went the following weekend.

The initial seminar took place in a large room that seated well over 100 beginners, where the rationale behind TM was explained. Then we were each assigned to a teacher, who would show us how to meditate and give us our special mantra. I waited my turn, then followed my teacher up to a small room in a distant corner of the building. "Close your eyes," he told me. "Breathe slowly and deeply. Repeat the mantra over and over in your head without trying. If you drift off and start daydreaming, gently bring yourself back to the mantra. And your mantra is….ee-mah'. Say it with me, with an emphasis on the second vowel. Ee-mah'."

Eemah. My mantra was eemah, the Hebrew word for mother.

Ohmygod, what was I going to do? Here I was, a Jewish boy from Brandeis by way of Orlando, and my mantra was eemah. Talk about ridiculous. Talk about reinforcing whatever mommy neuroses I had. I couldn't do it. I didn't know what to do. Could I ask for a different one? Could I start over? I was upset, terrified to question what I'd been taught. I was only 17. What did I know? After all, this was my mantra, selected especially for me. What did that say about me anyway? When I was given a mantra that was supposed to be mine and mine alone, I didn't know enough to say, "Please, in Hebrew that's mommy. Please, give me something else to meditate on."

What did I do? I got up and walked out, eemah rolling around in my head.

I didn't realize it then, but years later I understood that I'd been taught a lesson, an important lesson, and a Jewish one. Did I find my way through meditation? Did I spend years meditating on my mother, and figure out why the universe had asked me to meditate twice a day on one of the people I thought enough about anyway?

No. I sucked it up and asked Rick what to do, who laughed out loud and gave me some good advice. Finally, I'd run into someone who assumed I didn't know everything, someone who thought they knew better than me.

"That's crazy," he said. "You can't meditate on eemah. Pick your own mantra."

And that's what I did. I found one that fit me, and in that simple process, I took the first baby step toward becoming who I am. Meditation, for all its benefits and calming ways, may have been a misstep. I was running from my Judaism, running to anything exotic, anything extreme. And it didn't fit quite right. I was able to say no, that's not me. I'll find something that is. And it was that question that ultimately led me back to my roots, back to embracing my Jewishness, though that path, that discovery, took many more years.

So-hahm. I am that that I am. My mantra for life.

Great Love

My Aunt Rita Levy died last week. Of all the siblings in her family, she was perhaps the least well known. Her sister Dorothy (Dottie) Morrell was considered the gatekeeper to the Orlando Jewish Community for many years, greeting and introducing new residents to those who lived here, and the cultural series at the Jewish Community Center was named after her. Sister Florence (Flossie) Gluckman founded the Neighborhood Law Center in Orlando that served the poor and indigent for many years. Bea Ettinger began the Center for Continuing Education for Women, now run out of the University of Central Florida. And my father Jerry was many things to many people: a popular attorney and civil rights advocate, twice president of the Jewish Federation, president and one of the founders of Temple Israel, key to the establishment of the Kinneret Towers, subsidized housing apartments for low income seniors.

But if you asked people about Rita Levy – the original Rita Bornstein before my mother or the president of Rollins College – you heard no stories about community building or visionary leadership. What you heard about was love, and in particular, her lifelong love affair with her husband, my uncle Morton, who died of cancer many years ago.

There is no doubt that their relationship was a love for the ages, founded on depths and passion and strength that are uncommon nowadays. When he was a soldier overseas during World War II he wrote her a letter every day, profound letters that spoke to their love in ways and words far closer to Keats and Shelley and Yeats than any modern poetry. And after hearing it recounted again and again, by different voices with different expressions, I have pondered the meaning of great love a great deal, and while I have no great conclusions, I do have a greater understanding and appreciation for what it means to truly love.

Rita's son Dan, his wife Jane and daughters Hannah and Sadie were over at our house one night to visit, and the subject of this monumental relationship came up. Hannah, a bright young woman of 21, made the comment that she understood what it meant to love so deeply, to which I quickly (really too quickly) responded, "No you don't." And while I may have been hasty in my interruption, I was right in my thought, for there is no way someone so young can grasp the depth of devotion, but even more than that, the necessary level of commitment and sometimes desperate work one must do to maintain a great love.

When Ben Affleck said, at the Academy Awards, that his relationship with wife Jennifer Garner was work, many people gasped. But he couldn't have been more truthful or accurate. For love to endure it can't be ignored, forgotten, or assumed. It must be exercised, pored over, considered or it will go dormant and ultimately fade.

Whether we talk about a love of God, or our homeland or faith, the one thing I know, the one thing I am certain of, is that no love is easy. No love comes without effort. Even the spectacular love between my Uncle Morton and Aunt Rita must have had its ups and downs, its work, its conscious struggle to maintain. There must have been stressful times and depressing times, times of separation and disconnect, but in the end they never wavered in their resolve to be together, and that is why, when people spoke about my Aunt Rita at her funeral and service, they spoke with admiration bordering on veneration. And it is why I can say, beyond a doubt, that I understand what it means to have a great love, because I have one of my own.

I have only been married once, and that is all I will be married. This week, as my wife approaches a landmark birthday, I look up to her with awe and devotion and appreciation for all that our love has been, good and bad, easy and difficult. We married when she was a young woman of 22 and I a grizzled old 29, and it took us many years of serious, hard work and innumerable daily experiences and joy and suffering and a constant commitment to being together to make our love what it is. This is the tip of the iceberg, the barest I can offer to describe my love, born of friendship and passion, blood and sweat and stains and scars and cast in ribbons of steel and ice. To my best friend and lifelong love, this is all I am, and all I am is yours.

After Life

My brother died in Seattle early in the evening on September 19, 2006, just before Rosh Hashana. I was sitting in the parking lot of his hospital, taking a moment to listen to an obscure song by an little known alternative band when I got a call that he had passed away. The song was titled "Brother" by The Annuals. I missed him by minutes. Coincidence that I was listening to that song while his spirit left the earth? Probably.

But then the following night, after I had flown back to Orlando with Ray's body, and my wife and I had gone to bed and fallen into a light, disjointed sleep, she suddenly popped up, wide awake, and told me, "I just had the strangest dream. I was at the funeral home standing by Ray's coffin. The coffin was open and I could see him lying there. All of a sudden he sat up and looked at me and said, "Tell Eric I'm ok."

The Eric he referred to had to be our cousin Eric Peisner. "That's weird," I replied. "Have you ever dreamed about Eric before?"

"No," she said. "I'll have to tell him." I agreed, and the next day, after the funeral when we all returned to our house, she found Eric and conveyed the gist of the dream. We expected he would be mildly surprised, pleased at the connection Pat made between him and Ray, but he was stunned. His head jerked back. He looked, literally, like he'd seen a ghost.

"Ray and I made a deal years ago," he told us. "Whichever one went first was supposed to send the other a signal if there was something after life." Pat gasped. My eyes opened wide. We knew nothing of the compact they'd made. The signal had been sent and delivered.

Now fast forward to November, 2013. My mother died on November 18. The next day I was with my wife, my sister, and my brother-in-law, getting a quick lunch at Whole Foods before meeting with our rabbi. We'd just left my mother's apartment, where we'd been cleaning and organizing. At the food bar I ran into a member of our Jewish community, a woman a few years younger than I, whose brother had been one of my brother's good friends. I had not seen or spoken to her in years. Running into her there was entirely coincidental. She asked me how my family was, how my mother was doing. "Strange you should ask," I replied. "The family's ok, but my mother passed away last night."

She took a step back, the color draining from her face as it had Eric's. "Really?" she said, out of breath.

"Yes, why?"

"I had a dream with her in it last night. She was wearing a red blouse, standing in line waiting to see a movie."

"Have you ever dreamed about her before?" I asked. I thought maybe this wasn't so unusual. My mother had taught many children in Sunday School and at the community Hebrew High School program. Maybe she'd had dreams like this before. Maybe my mother was some sort of symbolic figure for her.

"No, never," she replied. "Never."

Standing in line to see a movie....about what? Her life? Her life to come? Coincidence that I ran into her at Whole Foods? That we spoke? That she asked about my mother, and told me about a dream she'd had? I don't think so. I think something else was going on.

Now lest anyone think I'm a quack, some overly metaphysical soul-searching mystic, rest assured. I'm not. At best I see the world in shades of gray. I have many questions and few answers. Doubt rather than certainty fills my mind. And yet I'm left dumbfounded by these spiritual coincidences that can't possibly be coincidences.

Of all the great insecurities we face as Jews, perhaps there is none so great as the one we deal with regarding what happens when we die. In Judaism there is no emphasis on heaven or hell. It's all about living life to the best and fullest while we're here. My mother was convinced we simply vanish into the void, and was frightened of the oblivion she faced until her last few days, when she seemed to accept everything. My brother wanted to believe in reincarnation, thought it existed in some form or other. We are taught that our souls are unique and precious and return to God when we die. I have an image in my mind of a giant universal soul, that when we expire that spark of energy that made us who we are, that bit of cosmic soul returns home. Perhaps as it goes it leaves a trail, a message for the more sensitive to pick up. Perhaps when a child is born that new, perfect, unique soul is made of snippets and pieces of many souls, largely one, but parts of others, all part of that great godly energy. I have found a sort of uncertain, hesitant peace in contemplating this, and what awaits me now doesn't seem as scary.

For all of you who wonder and fret about death, for those of you who are elderly and facing your last days, or sick or wounded of just plain frightened of what happens when we die, I won't say don't. I won't be so foolish as to tell you I have the answer, that there's no reason to fear death, but I will tell you I believe there's more. Take comfort in that. I don't pretend to know what comes after life. I just think something does. I think something else awaits.

A Child's Jewish Christmas

A mother was trying to explain to her young son why he would be staying home during the High Holy Days. "It's because we're Jews and these are very important holidays," she told him. "We'll go to synagogue for services and have special meals with family and friends, and God will write our names in the Book of Life for another year."

He mulled this information over. "Is anyone else in my class skipping school and going to services?" he asked.

"No," she replied. "You're the only Jewish child in your class." At that he burst into tears.

"What's wrong, honey?" she asked, trying to console him. "What's upsetting you?"

He choked out his words. "That means I'll be the only kid in school on Christmas!"

A young girl was feeling the peer pressure exerted on her by her close friends. They all wanted to ride their bikes downtown to see Santa after school. This was old Orlando, when it was safe to ride to the drugstore for a sundae or be out of your parents' attention for hours at a time. It was Friday, and the holidays were approaching, and all the other girls in the neighborhood were planning to ride to see Santa and tell him what they wanted for Christmas. But she was Jewish, and had never sat in Santa's lap before, and didn't feel quite right about it. What would she say? Would she ask for anything, even though she didn't celebrate Christmas? Or would she just stand on the sidelines while her girlfriends chatted with Santa, feeling once more like an outcast, part of the group but not? She wanted to be part of things. She wanted to belong. And they were relentless. Come on, they cajoled her. Come with us. It'll be fun. We're all going. And finally she gave in, and rode downtown with her friends.

In this case, she decided, she wasn't going to be left out just because she was Jewish. She would go the whole way. She would sit in Santa's lap and ask for what she wanted. She didn't have to say it would be for Chanukah instead of Christmas. She'd just ask. So she waited her turn, and when it came she dutifully approached the man who looked like all the pictures she'd ever seen of Santa Claus. Big belly. White beard. Red suit. She climbed into his lap, but before she could say anything he noticed the Jewish star – the Mogen David – hanging around her neck.

"Little girl," he said. "What are you doing here? It's Shabbos!"

She rode home, exhilarated. "Mommy!" she cried when she opened the front door and raced inside. "Santa's Jewish!"

In both instances an innocent child honestly misinterpreted some basic information about themselves and the holidays. In both cases they wanted to fit in, to be part of the crowd. But where one ended in tears and one in laughter, where one felt more detached and one more a part, ultimately, as their parents sat down with them and explained in greater detail how and why they were different, they came to a deeper understanding of what it means to be a Jew in a Christian world.

And that is the lesson to us as parents in both these tales. It's not about competing with a Christian world. It's about recognizing our children's needs to both be part of the world and to acknowledge what sets us apart. It's not about the gifts, or the lights, or the trees, or being the only kid in school on Christmas, or whether or not Santa is a Jew. It's about listening to our children's view of the world, helping them to grasp it, and then to accept who they are. We all have our place, after all. Sometimes we just need a little help figuring out where it is.

The Rabbi's Yad

My life, these days, is surrounded by bar mitzvahs, and not necessarily my son's. And it seems that with each bar (or bat) mitzvah I attend, I am struck by something new. Something different. This past weekend I was hit hard, in the most surprising way.

I attended my first ever orthodox service. The first in my life, which in and of itself is shocking. The service was both the same and not the same as what I'm used to. The prayers were the same. So were the melodies, though they were sung differently. My synagogue's services are more orderly. Prayers are chanted in unison. At the orthodox service the prayers were sung more chaotically, each person chanting at their own pace. Neither way is better. Neither is worse. They are just different. The same is true of the service itself. My synagogue, while warm and friendly, has a gentle formality to it. This shul was casual, conversational, with the rabbi walking up to people, giving cues, commenting, asking questions, and the members, in turn, treating the service as much like a family dinner as a religious experience. Again, no better or worse. Just different. My synagogue is large. This one is small. I could go on, but you get my point.

One of my son's close friends celebrated his bar mitzvah. But this isn't about that. Not about the maftir, or the haftorah, or the speech. It's about the rabbi's son. Now I don't know Rabbi Dubov. We've met many times over the years, but I can't say I've ever had a lengthy conversation with him. But he knows my name and I know his. He greeted me and my son Gabriel warmly. I liked his sermon. I didn't know one of his children, a little eight year old boy, has Down's Syndrome.

The boy was all over his father during the service, walking around the sanctuary, coming up to the rabbi, pulling him down to his level to say something or ask something, standing on a folding chair next to his father as the rabbi read torah. I was impressed by what a good, patient father the rabbi is. I was equally impressed by how accommodating the shul's members were to the boy. But I was moved by what happened while the rabbi read torah.

Tradition dictates that the reader use a yad, a pointer often made of metal to follow the words, both to show respect to the torah by not touching it and to show respect to the person who has an aliyah, so they can see the words and follow along. But in this case, not all the time but often, as the boy stood on a chair by his rabbi father, watching the torah and listening to the chanting, the rabbi used his son's finger as his yad, holding the boy's hand and following the words with a living pointer.

What went through this little boy's head as his finger followed the words? Did he feel a special connection to his father, to the service and the torah reading? What was the rabbi thinking? What was his intent? Was it something special they'd worked out together? Or was he simply including his son in the service?

As is often the case at an orthodox synagogue, the torah service took place in the center of the sanctuary, not at the front on the bimah, and I sat with my son two rows away, watching the rabbi guide his son's tiny fingers across the scroll. And what I thought, rightly or wrongly as I watched, was that maybe the rabbi was doing that because he knew in doing so he was closer to God, and so was his boy. I think maybe he knew that his son's finger, following scripture, was as close as anyone on earth could come to union with the holy. I think that together, aware of it or not, they brought a unique, reverential spirit into the building. I know they did for me, as I watched a father, a son, a rabbi and a little boy reach out together to try and touch God.

www.ingramcontent.com/pod-product-compliance
Lightning Source LLC
Chambersburg PA
CBHW070624130626
46556CB00001B/470